T0087192

HOW TO SUCCEED IN COLLEGE
(While Really Trying)

CHICAGO GUIDES TO ACADEMIC LIFE

HOW TO SUCCEED IN COLLEGE

(While Really Trying)

A Professor's Inside Advice

JON B. GOULD

The University of Chicago Press

Chicago and London

The University of Chicago Press, Chicago 60637
The University of Chicago Press, Ltd., London
© 2012 by The University of Chicago
All rights reserved. Published 2012.
Printed in the United States of America

22 21 20 19 18 17 16 15   5 6 7

ISBN-13: 978-0-226-30465-6 (cloth)
ISBN-13: 978-0-226-30466-3 (paper)
ISBN-10: 0-226-30465-5 (cloth)
ISBN-10: 0-226-30466-3 (paper)

Library of Congress Cataloging in Publication Data
Gould, Jon B.
How to succeed in college (while really trying): a professor's
inside advice / Jon B. Gould.
p. cm.
Includes bibliographical references and index.
ISBN-13: 978-0-226-30465-6 (hardcover : alkaline paper)
ISBN-13: 978-0-226-30466-3 (paperback : alkaline paper)
ISBN-10: 0-226-30465-5 (hardcover : alkaline paper)
ISBN-10: 0-226-30466-3 (paperback : alkaline paper)
1. Educational counseling—Handbooks, manuals, etc.
2. Counseling in higher education—Handbooks,
manuals, etc.   I. Title.
LB1027.5.G635 2012
378.1′98—dc23
2011037291

♾ This paper meets the requirements of ANSI/NISO Z39.48–1992
(Permanence of Paper).

FOR MICHAEL AND EMILY,

from whom I learn more every day

CONTENTS

ACKNOWLEDGMENTS

How many people are still in regular touch with their seventh grade social studies teachers nearly thirty-five years after graduating middle school? In my case, I have been nurtured and mentored by several excellent teachers. That social studies teacher, Chuck Meyers, opened my eyes to the world and helped to sharpen my increasing interest in current events. Like all good teachers, he challenged me to see things through different perspectives and encouraged me along a path of additional exploration with a wonderfully dry sense of humor. I often wonder if I would be where I am today without his influence. Fortunately, I have not had to worry.

I'm certain I would not have become a good instructor without the involvement and example of several excellent teachers. Besides Chuck, H. W. Perry, Kim Scheppele, and Gerry Rosenberg showed me early on what it meant to be an excellent professor. Each has since become a friend and mentor, and, in fact, I owe my first book to Gerry's careful guidance. So, too, Vic Ferrall, my former boss and past president of Beloit College, has been a shining defender of the liberal arts and an example of what higher education can realize.

Closer to home, my in-laws, Marlene and Haskell Springer, were themselves university professors before retiring, and each has helped me to understand how excellent teaching can be effectively paired with meaningful scholarship. Even more dear, my parents nurtured a sense of inquisitiveness and were always proud observers—and even enthusiastic participants—when they came to see me teach. On one such occasion, a student approached my mother after class. Handing her a copy of his recently graded bluebook, he playfully implored, "Can't you tell your son to grade me more leniently?" Mom took the exam, quickly read my comments in the back, and responded with a wry smile, "It looks like you should be spending more time preparing for your next exam and less time complaining about this one." Apparently, the apple doesn't fall far from the tree.

I have had the privilege of teaching at several institutions as a professor. I am thankful to many colleagues who have helped to improve my teaching and who offered stories and examples that have made their way into this book. Although I am reluctant to single out particular individuals among such a long list of helpful peers, two professors deserve special mention. James Willis and Devon Johnson, my former colleagues at George Mason University and both winners of the university's teaching award, have been inspirational examples. Although they would modestly claim otherwise, I have learned much from them and consider both to be among higher education's finest teachers.

There are several people who helped to bring this book to fruition. I am grateful to the anonymous reviewers for the University of Chicago Press, whose helpful comments and suggestions improved the manuscript. John Gilliom, my favorite scholar-farmer, provided invaluable support and feedback along the way. I trust he (and his darling youngest daughter) will be satisfied that I mentioned Haverford College in the book. At the University of Chicago Press, I am indebted to Mary Gehl for her excellent and wry editing, to Liz Fischer for help in marketing the book, and to Rodney Powell for years of troubleshooting.

This book owes to the vision and leadership of one person—John Tryneski, my friend and editor at the University of Chicago Press. I have yet to find a person so universally admired and respected in university publishing as John, plaudits he so richly deserves. I recall sitting with John on a bench at the annual meeting of the Law and Society Association. We were talking about one of my then "problem students," a smart and engaging student who didn't seem to understand what his professors were expecting of him. As we got further into the conversation, John turned to me and issued what proved to be a prophetic challenge—"I wonder if there is a book in this?"

I'm delighted to report that the student is now a practicing lawyer, and, of course, the book is now done. The latter truly owes to John's guidance, feedback, support, and occasional accommodations when the rest of my life got in the way. I have learned a great deal from John— about how to write and think better, but more importantly, about how to treat others decently. As I say repeatedly in this book, some of the most influential experiences in college take place outside of the classroom. In my own life, my friendship with John Tryneski has been one of the most rewarding.

Of course, one relationship stands supreme in my life—that with my greatest supporter and life's love, Ann. I know for sure that my life would not work without her, and there really aren't sufficient words to convey my thanks and appreciation for all she does. As you begin your path through adulthood, be on the lookout for someone who makes you laugh, who brings energy and joie de vivre to your life, who challenges you to consider different perspectives, who will be there for you on the good days and the bad ones too, and who helps to make you a better person. If you are fortunate to find someone like this, grab on tightly. It's a heck of a ride.

INTRODUCTION

I love the start of the semester. As I step to the podium for that first class, I usually look out over a sea of expectant faces, students well rested, eager to be there, and with high hopes for the course. For the majority of students, the semester will end well. They will come to class regularly, do the reading, participate in class discussions, and perform well on their exams and papers. As a result, their final grades will be respectable, if not quite good.

Inevitably, however, the end of the semester will find at least one disappointed student sitting in my office commiserating about why he did not perform as well in class as he wished. It's a meeting we both dread, a conference I call the "if only" conversation. "If only I had started my term paper earlier," "if only I had studied longer for the exam," "if only I hadn't been so busy with fraternity rush," the student tells me, he could have earned a better grade and learned more in the class. Now well into my second decade as a professor, I have heard many of these explanations over the years. As sympathetic as I am to the students' plight, it's gotten to the point where I've added a line to syllabi reminding students at the beginning of the term that "your grade will be a record of what you do in this class—not what you could have, should have, or would have done had circumstances been different."

My colleagues and I talk about these students when we meet in the halls or in the faculty lounge. "If only this student had known how to study better, she would have done well in my class," we sigh. "If only that student had recognized what was being asked on the exam, he would have aced it," we lament. No responsible faculty member wants to see students struggle, but when we talk privately, we are amazed that some students make college so difficult for themselves. Academic life should not be a mystery, and yet too many students come to college either not recognizing what will be expected of them or unprepared to meet the new challenges that await them.

The problem is surprising given the cottage industry in college preparation in the United States. Any college-bound high school student is undoubtedly familiar with the excess of books designed to advise them on their options for college. By my count there are nearly fifty books available with advice on how to choose and gain admission to college. Once admitted, however, the number of guidebooks for college students narrows considerably. Some offer advice—much of it tongue-in-cheek—about "what college is really like," from recommendations for choosing a roommate to tales of Greek rush and reviews of the "hookup scene" on campus. Others focus on academics, but even here the options are few and generally fall into two camps. The larger category envisions college academics as a game; these guides generally are written by former students advising the next generation about how to cram for tests or where to look for collections of old exams. A smaller collection is written by faculty who typically cover pedagogical research. Although interesting to some, these books are generally directed to fellow professors who may wish to revamp the strategies they employ in the classroom.

Largely missing among these books is a guidebook for college students written by the very person who will teach and grade them: a professor. After all, we're the ones responsible for the academic program. We do the teaching and advising, and at the end of four years we'll be the ones waving our graduates goodbye with letters of recommendation and highest hopes for their success. We also appreciate the allures of the cocurricular side of college life, the realization that for many students the challenge of college is not simply keeping up with the academic requirements but also learning how to take charge of their own lives as adults. College asks a lot of students that high schoolers never had to face: how to balance study with play when no one will tell you when and how much you must study; how to live with someone you don't know; in some cases, how to cook for yourself and do your own laundry and cleaning; how to keep up with a larger amount of reading and writing, especially when a deeper level of comprehension and understanding is required; and, perhaps most importantly, how to get the most out of an education and experience that may be costing you or your parents upwards of a quarter of a million dollars over four years.

Why to Read This Book

This book seeks to takes the mystery out of college life from the perspective of a professor. In the chapters that follow I describe the various academic requirements of college, explain what faculty members expect of students in completing these assignments, and provide specific strategies to help students excel at their academic work. I also offer advice for students in balancing academic life with their cocurricular activities, work obligations, and free time. The book does not promise a secret formula to ace every class, but students who read this guide and follow its recommendations will be better prepared to succeed in any college course. They will be ready from their first day on campus to get the most out of their time and money. Among the subjects addressed are how to identify good teachers that will make class interesting; how and when to choose your classes and major; developing strategies for note taking and reading so that you understand what is being conveyed; understanding quizzes and tests so you recognize what professors are asking from you; proven approaches for writing good essays, including tips on how to avoid common pitfalls; guidance on when to seek help if you're having problems; and advice on how to exploit untapped resources on campus that many students don't know about.

Ultimately, this is a book for students and their families to demystify the college experience so that you get the most out of your investment. Think of it this way: if someone suddenly handed you a nest egg to invest over four years, you would undoubtedly investigate the investment options before you wrote a check. That is the basis behind the college advising industry. As soon as you took the PSAT or ACT announcing your interest in attending college, you likely were bombarded with brochures and catalogs on the various options for collegiate study. You and your parents may well have read college guides or even conducted campus visits to help you decide what college to attend. But once you arrive on campus the real challenge of meeting the expectations of college begins. This book will give you a head start in understanding what will be asked of you, explaining the process of college study and offering specific strategies to help you excel as a college student. All of us on campus want to see you do your best and make the most out of your years with us. This book will help you to do just that and enjoy college.

About Me

One of the things we will teach you in college is the importance of being a critical consumer of information. "Why should you believe this author?" is a question you will hear countless times in your classes. The same should be true of this book. After all, you don't know me. Why is my advice any more valuable than that of your Aunt Sally who attended your same school twenty years ago? These are questions you should keep in mind when anyone wants to give you advice on college, whether about your initial choice of school or the classes or major you select.

I have been a professor for almost two decades now, in positions as varied as a law instructor at the University of Chicago, a political science teacher at Beloit College and San Jose State University, a faculty member at George Mason University, and now a professor of public affairs at American University in Washington, D.C. I have been a graduate teaching assistant, an adjunct instructor, a term professor, and am presently a tenured full professor. I've taught in a lot of different environments—small seminars at a liberal arts college, lecture halls seating hundreds of first-year university students, and clinical courses in which students test classroom theories against experience in the field. I also have been recognized for my teaching. I've published articles in academic journals about college instruction, and I've won a university teaching award. Along the way, I've seen what works—the study skills that help students understand and retain information, the strategies for test taking that best answer exam questions, and the general approach to college that allows students to get the most out of their education.

The other reason to trust my advice is that I'm willing to share. It is surprising how few professors take the time to talk with their students about how they can succeed in a class, let alone at college. Some of us, I suspect, believe that the secrets to college are self-evident. "They all succeeded at high school or they wouldn't be here," some of my colleagues say about their students. "They already should know what to do—complete the reading, come to class and take notes, study before exams." Certainly, these are necessary ingredients for college success, but they alone are not sufficient. What some of my colleagues forget is that for most college students, classes are but one part of the experience. Students are balancing a host of new responsibilities and face heightened pressures as well when they take their families' money and expectations with them to college. We faculty can miss the proverbial forest for the trees sometimes, becoming fixated on the material in our respective syllabi rather than sharing those skills and experiences that students should acquire over a college career. Professors all have a sense of these—after all, that's why faculty write curricula. But we assume too readily that students understand these expectations as readily as we do.

Structure of the Book

This book lets you in on the secrets that faculty know about college but sometimes are reluctant to share. It is a resource you should keep on your shelves to consult as you wind your way through your college career. The book itself is divided into six chapters. In chapter 1, I give an overview of college, explaining how it is different from high school and describing what is expected of you. This chapter also introduces those who will teach you—the faculty—and describes the various types of instructors you may encounter, their roles, strengths, and weaknesses, and offers tips on how to identify the best teachers. With this information under your belt, you'll be better able to step foot on campus that first day confident that you'll know where to begin.

Chapter 2 discusses the academic program, helping you understand what courses you must take, determine what classes you want to take, and give you the tools to balance them. This chapter offers tips on courses and majors and provides practical advice for choosing classes that are useful, interesting, and engaging.

Chapter 3 will help prepare you for what's expected in class, giving you strategies for how to handle the reading, remain an active participant in class, and stay on top of course requirements. You may think you already know how to do this, having succeeded in high school, but the heightened and diverse expectations of college present new challenges that require their own approaches.

Chapter 4 addresses exams, while chapter 5 covers papers, helping you understand what your professors expect from you and providing techniques to do your best on these assignments. Among other things, these chapters outline strategies for effective studying and writing, including timelines and examples of typical problems to avoid.

Chapter 6 will help you to weather academic or personal difficulties that may arise in college. Almost every college has resources for students in need, and there is no shame in asking for help. The real tragedy is watching a student struggle along the downward curve toward failure when, with a little intervention, she could have succeeded. This chapter explains where to seek help on campus and, perhaps more importantly, provides some telltale signs of when it's time to seek assistance. Finally, it considers college from the perspective of your eventual goal—commencement into an exciting job or graduate school. It's a big "real world" into which we'll eventually send you, and the prospects of adjusting to life on your own may seem treacherous. Thus, this chapter provides tips on the transition, including how to utilize faculty and college resources in making the jump. For those students who have not had enough of academic life—or who someday may want to return for additional training—the book also offers advice on how to prepare for graduate school.

I should say at the outset that this book does not purport to provide "the answer" to college success. You should be wary of any advice that claims to be foolproof or exclusive. If nothing else, one of the goals of college is to teach critical thinking, and I encourage you to consider and question the advice contained in this book. I've been at this a while and am confident that you will find the guidance helpful in your college career, but you should evaluate the recommendations through the lens of your own experience. College is an exciting opportunity. Take the time now to make the most out of it.

1

WELCOME TO CAMPUS

Why Go to College?

More than 40 years ago, there were 2,329 colleges and universities, approximately 1 for every 85,000 Americans. Today, there are well over 4,000 schools, the ratio dropping to 1 for every 75,000 Americans. In fact, the percentage of Americans who graduated college has jumped nearly threefold over that period to reach 28 percent of those over 25 years old.[1] Colleges have diversified as well. At the start of the civil rights movement, African Americans constituted fewer than 5 percent of the entering freshmen class. By 2007, that figure was up to 13 percent, roughly mirroring the percentage of African Americans in the U.S. population.[2] Women, especially, are attending college and graduate school in record numbers. Female students now outnumber their male counterparts at every level of postsecondary education except in doctoral programs.[3]

All around there are signs that college is more welcoming to Americans of all stripes. Gone are the days when only the rich and well-connected attended college. Today, three-quarters of college enrollment occurs at state institutions, where, not coincidentally, tuition is lower.[4] Our colleges and universities also are the envy of the world. According to the Department of Education, foreign enrollment at U.S. schools continues to rise, hitting a record of over 600,000 students in the 2007–2008 academic year. "In today's competitive international environment," a State Department representative says, "the increase in enrollments . . . demonstrates again that the U.S. remains the premier destination for international students."[5]

This is all well and good, but the looming question for prospective students like yourself is whether college is right for *you*. Do you need a college degree to succeed in life? How valuable is a college education? The trick is separating the two questions. Contrary to what you will hear from most high school guidance counselors, a college degree is not an absolute requirement for professional success. It's more like the multivitamin you may take. Will it absolutely prevent a cold? No, not by itself, but it certainly helps.

Census surveys continue to show that college graduates earn more than those who do not attend college; the most recent figures reflect a 2:1 difference. The salary gap widens with even more education. According to 2005 census data, "workers with an advanced degree [earned] an average of $74,602, and those without a high school diploma [averaged] $18,734."[6] But these data may obscure the fact that college students are a self-selecting lot. As one critic explains, "You could lock the college-bound in a closet for four years, and they'd still go on to earn more than the pool of non-college-bound—they're brighter, more motivated, and have better family connections."[7] Consider that some of the wealthiest members of society have dropped out of college to start their own businesses. Bill Gates, a creator of Microsoft; Larry Ellison, who cofounded Oracle; Steve Jobs, the innovator behind Apple; and Michael Dell, whose computer company bears his name, all made millions without a college degree. If you're motivated, have an entrepreneurial streak, and can create a winning business plan, perhaps college isn't necessary for you.

My guess, though, is that this description applies to just a handful of eighteen-year-olds. For most of us, a college degree is a prerequisite for many of the higher-paying jobs in society. Plumbers and auto mechanics earn an enviable wage, electricians and computer technicians are in demand, but unless you're prepared to start your own business and make money as an entrepreneur, most of the jobs that pay best require that college sheepskin.

I hate to lead with money as the justification for college, but there is no denying the fact that college is expensive. The average "list price" for private college tuition in 2007 was over $20,000 a year, with public schools averaging a little more than $6,000.[8] Taken over four years, you could buy several luxury cars or put a down payment on a house for what you or your parents will spend on college tuition. The question, of course, is whether college is worth this amount.

Why College Is Worth It

You hardly will be surprised to hear that I think it is—but not because college lends itself to a ready cost-benefit analysis. We're not selling automobiles; we're in the business of hope. I first heard this expression from my mother-in-law, who served as a college president. Certainly, President Obama has spoken about "the audacity of hope," a "belief in things not seen, a belief that there are better days ahead."[9] The line may make for good politics, but it also holds true in American higher education.

Anyone who sets foot on campus arrives with hope in her eyes—the hope for a better life. For some students that will be measured in raw dollars, their internal actuaries calculating how much more they will earn over a lifetime with a college degree. Other students hope to improve their social standing, the white-collar world of a college degree being more appealing than the life they have known. For others, college is about skill development, learning how to think and communicate better. And for another group, college is about expanding one's mind and experiences, from exposure to new ideas in the classroom to the growth that occurs from living in the dorms with someone of a different ethnic background. None of these motives is exclusive, for most students come to campus with a variety of goals. Professors understand this, even if we would prefer to envision our students enrolling simply for the love of learning.

Is hope naive or, even worse, elitist? Just the contrary. Go to New York Harbor sometime and read Emma Lazarus's inscription on the statue that lit the way for many of our immigrant ancestors: "Give me your tired, your poor / Your huddled masses yearning to breathe free." America is all about hope—the hope that dreams will bring a brighter future—just as American higher education is about the hope of a more rewarding, meaningful, and even profitable life. College is elitist, but not for the reasons you may think. We're not sitting around in our ivory towers sipping sherry in tweed jackets tsk-tsking about the unwashed masses. That image is best left to Hollywood's B movies. Rather, we're trying to will the best out of life—a better understanding of human behavior to make life more rewarding, scientific and medical discoveries to improve conditions on the ground, and meaningful interactions to enhance personal insight.

Sure, on the hierarchy of human needs, education is not a top priority, ranking above such basic necessities as food, water, security, and belonging. But civilized societies are concerned about people's higher needs, including esteem and fulfillment, and education is directly tied to each of them. College is a place to grow, to nurture your skills, to develop confidence in your abilities, and to put yourself on the path to an interesting and engaged future. It's hardly a wonder that 89 percent of college graduates in a national poll said the experience was worth the expense.[10] It's the "goofy and formative experiences" of college, as one recent graduate put it, that make the experience so worthwhile.

Many Paths to College

College, of course, is not for everyone. If you were a poor student in high school, the academic demands of a traditional four-year school may be too much at first. If you lack the motivation to study hard and keep up in class, then those tuition dollars likely will be wasted. Or, perhaps the idea of spending four years of your youth caught up in books and classes sounds like punishment. But my hunch is that at some point in your life you will start wondering, "Is this all there is?" You'll go to work, hang out with your friends, look after your family, and this will be fine for a while. But over time you may get dissatisfied, feel closed in, want to expand your horizons. That is where college comes in. Whether you test the waters with a single class in your field or jump into a new degree path, hope and curiosity are likely to get the better of you. Hope of expanding your career possibilities, curiosity about new ideas, and both as you envision a better life for yourself.

There are many paths to colleges, not all of them a direct line from high school to college hall. Even if you think you are unprepared for college study—and research shows that an embarrassing number of admitted students are lacking[11]—there are options to making it in a four-year college. Some students begin first in a community college, building a solid base of academic skills before transferring. Others take advantage of writing and learning skills centers on campus. These and other options are described in greater detail in chapter 6. For now, let me at least plant the seed that college *can* be for anyone who is motivated, curious, and willing to work hard. With plenty of financial aid options available at most schools, the only real roadblock to a college education is discipline and dedication.

How Is College Different than High School?

If you have been admitted to college, especially if the admissions process was competitive, you were likely a good student in high school. That's the good news; you're almost assuredly capable of being a competent college student. But college is different than high school in so many ways. There are all of the social adjustments to make—living on your own (if your school is residential) and perhaps far from home, taking responsibility for your own needs, and making new friends. Looking around campus, the student body may also appear to be quite different from your high school class. If the admissions office has done its job well, your college classmates will be a diverse lot, encompassing different races and ethnicities, family backgrounds, and opinions. Learning to navigate among such diversity is one of the unique challenges of college.

Perhaps most significantly, academic life can be quite different from what you were accustomed to in high school. The first difference is that you will spend much less time in class in college. If you were like most high school students, you had to attend class for about six hours per day. Of course, you may have had some free periods, but you were generally expected to be in or around the high school building, if not in class, for about thirty hours each week. In college, you will likely spend about half that time in class. Most college students take between twelve and eighteen credit hours of classes each semester. A credit hour is a rough approximation for how often a class meets each week. So a fifteen-hour course load—which you generally must average each semester to graduate in four years—translates to fifteen hours of class each week, or three hours per day if you were to take classes each day of the week.

Many college students (and, ahem, several professors as well) try to arrange their schedules so that they do not have to take classes on Fridays, but even if you're squeezing those fifteen hours of class into four days each week, it still has you registered for a little less than four hours of class per day. Remember that thing called the eight-hour work day? You're looking at a class schedule that will have you in class for half of that time, and that's not even taking classes a full five days per week.

I can hear parents cringing about now, wondering just how much partying their children will squeeze into the remaining twenty-five hours in a typical work week. The truth, however, is that college is structured so that for every hour a student spends in class she should have another two hours of preparation to keep up with the material. That means reading, writing papers, and studying for exams. So actually, the free time is not as plentiful as it first might appear. A student taking fifteen hours of coursework is looking at another fifteen to thirty hours per week of preparation outside of class. That adds up to thirty to forty-five hours of schoolwork each week. Suddenly, college looks more like a full-time job. But what makes college work different from a job, or even high school, is that students have the freedom to "time shift." If you would rather play Ultimate Frisbee in the afternoon and study late at night, that's your choice. If you want to go to a party and then stay up the rest of the night to complete a paper, you can try that as well. There is no reputable professor who would recommend this strategy (more on that later), but the point is that college students have tremendous freedom to structure their days as they please.

Ah, but here is the rub: just as you have the freedom to choose when to study or, indeed, whether to study at all, no one is going to run around with a net waiting to catch you if you fall. At some smaller schools the faculty may monitor your progress and even intervene if they see you falling behind, but no one will stand over you insisting that you complete your assignments or appear in class prepared for the day's material. This is a virtual certainty if you attend a large university where professors do not keep close tabs on your performance.

This doesn't mean that we don't care. Just the opposite—we all would like to see you succeed. But in a class of a hundred or more students, we do not have the time to mentor each of you personally, nor should we be expected to assume a responsibility that, in college, is yours. If you would like to play around that's your prerogative, but do not expect a professor to rescue you from yourself at the end of the term when you have not attended class or have failed to turn in the assignments. Illness and family emergencies are one thing, which generally will earn students a deserved extension, but irresponsibility will get you nowhere. Ask your parents about the scene in the movie *Animal House*, in which John Belushi's character receives the news that he is being expelled for a grade point average of 0. "Seven years of college down the drain" is not a line you want to hear yourself uttering, and I assure you that your parents are even less excited at the prospect. So one of the first challenges you must recognize about college is that it's up to you. If you go to class, if you do the reading and take notes, if you complete your assignments on time, then you are likely to prosper in college. But—and I'll say it again—the responsibility is yours.

What Is a Professor?

You'll also find a difference in who is standing at the front of the college classroom teaching you. Contrary to high school, where you may have been taught mainly by women, many of your college professors will be male. Most, too, have earned a PhD in a substantive discipline. Your high school teacher, by contrast, may have had a bachelor's or master's degree in the subject she taught—or in a completely different field— and, depending on the state, she may have needed additional classes in educational theory and practice in order to earn a teaching certificate. College professors face no such requirements. In fact, one of the little secrets of college is that few professors receive much preparation in teaching before they first head into the classroom.

The situation varies by the kind of college involved. Small liberal arts colleges, which market themselves on the availability of personal instruction, often spend considerable time coaching their new faculty in teaching. But at large universities—where the appeal is breadth of subjects and famous researchers—professors are sometimes thrown into the classroom right out of their doctoral programs without any mentoring or preparation on teaching. The reasons seem to be twofold. First, faculty at large universities are rewarded for their research more than their teaching. Rare, in fact, is the research university that takes teaching into account to the same degree as research when promoting faculty. Second, academe seems to assume that new professors have picked up the secrets of teaching by observation while they were graduate students. The logic, of course, is shaky, but at several large universities faculty receive too little preparation.

This is not to say that faculty at large universities are poor teachers. Many—because they are naturally interested in the process of learning—figure out how to be effective instructors. Some come to this naturally. Some even work at universities that have come to recognize the importance of training and mentoring faculty members in the art of instruction. But it would not be surprising to find that the great researcher, the faculty member who has won national prizes for his publications, is actually a mediocre instructor in the classroom.

This is not necessarily unreasonable. What your high school teachers never faced was the pressure to conduct research and publish findings in addition to teaching you. At every university, and at many liberal arts colleges as well, faculty are also expected to advance knowledge through their own research. Indeed, as I have said, this is the first priority at many schools. Young faculty members are often hired on what is known as a tenure track, meaning that they are working toward a process five or six years down the road in which the school will decide whether to keep them permanently, a process known as tenure. Faculty who receive tenure are afforded a number of job protections that insulate them from outside pressures while pursuing their scholarship. But to receive tenure, professors must spend considerable time conducting research, writing up the results, and submitting their papers and book manuscripts to be considered for publication.

What Faculty Do

You have undoubtedly heard the expression "publish or perish," which explains the pressures on young faculty members to conduct research and publish their findings or fail to be promoted. What you may not understand is the extent of those obligations. Most of us outside of liberal arts colleges are expected to publish two articles a year or one book every two to three years. But unlike those essays you've written in high school in which you cite various authors for their observations, professors are expected to generate new ideas or uncover original findings themselves. They must perform experiments, conduct surveys, review archival documents, or create entirely new theories, which they must then summarize in forty pages or so. But that's just the beginning, because they must also convince a peer-reviewed journal to publish their work. This is the most excruciating part of the publication process. A professor sends his article to a journal. The editor reads it first to decide whether it meets a threshold of originality and merit. If she thinks it reasonably promising, she'll then send it to two or three anonymous reviewers—other professors in the field—who will read the piece and comment upon the methods, findings, and presentation of the piece. Invariably, the reviewers will seek revisions in order for the piece to warrant publication, which actually is the good news, because in the majority of cases the journal will reject the piece for publication. So, the author must begin the process anew at another journal. It's a bit like book publishing, in which a promising new author must go through several rejections before finally finding a publishing house that will take a chance on her. Now, imagine having to do this twice a year for the rest of your career. Not so easy, huh?

Don't get me wrong. Almost all of us who are professors like our jobs. We have *chosen* this career because we value a life of the mind, because we treasure the independence to study what interests us and advocate for what we believe without censorship, and because we like teaching and training students. But this is not the breezy existence that some critics like to think we inhabit. Although, like our students, we have the ability to time shift—to work on that article at eleven o'clock at night rather than at two in the afternoon if we prefer—the work obligations are substantial and seem to grow each year. In my own case, I find myself busier as a professor that I was years ago as a lawyer. I'm also paid substantially less than I would have been had I continued in legal practice. But I'm in the classroom because I want to be, as are the vast majority of my colleagues you will meet in your academic career. So when you walk into your course that first day and look up at the lectern to see the face of your instructor, remember not only that we're trying to balance a lot in addition to teaching you but also that we are looking forward to spending the term with you. This is what we *want* do, not something that we must do.

The Liberal Ivory Tower

We might as well get one issue out of the way early. It is sometimes said that college faculty are a bunch of liberals who seek to indoctrinate their charges into similar ways of thinking. You may have read books or seen commentators on Fox News deriding campus radicals or ivory tower liberals. The truth is that college professors on the whole are more liberal than the general public. Ideology seems to vary with field of study—engineering and business professors are generally more conservative than are humanities or social sciences faculty, for example—but your professors likely will be more liberal than others you would encounter in a snapshot of the general public.

But this fact obscures an important point and glosses over the most important feature of faculty ideology. On the whole, college professors are no more liberal than are others of a similar educational level in society. It's been known for decades that a person's ideology varies with his educational level. People with modest education are more conservative than are those with high levels of formal education; those who have earned doctorates are the most liberal of all. Why is that so? We're not entirely sure. It may be that education leads to understanding and tolerance, both of which are features associated with liberalism. It also may be that the highly educated are encouraged to think critically about the world, to refuse to accept assumed truths, and to be open to change, all of which are associated with progressive views. Or, it could be that those with PhDs are less interested in lucrative careers and thus are more willing to endorse redistributive policies. Be that as it may, many faculty at many schools are likely to be left of center.

That *does not* mean, however, that liberal professors are seeking to convert disciples, that they reward liberal students or penalize conservative views in their classrooms. No responsible professor would ever push his ideology on others. The best professors don't even let their students know their views on partisan issues for fear that the knowledge might deter some students from offering an opposing view. One of the greatest compliments I have ever received as a teacher was from a student who told me that she did not know until after the semester was over what my political affiliation might be—and even then she only learned it when she came to babysit my children one night and caught sight of the bumper sticker on my wife's car that advertised a political candidate.

Challenging Yourself

What we're trying to do in the classroom is challenge each student to examine his views and think more thoroughly and coherently about what he truly believes. I regularly tell my students:

> If you come out of college believing what you did coming in, that's fine so long as you challenged yourself by opening up those views to other opinions. But if you leave the university having not aired out those beliefs, then not only have you missed the point of being here, but you also leave yourself vulnerable outside of college. A person who hasn't examined his own views cannot know where the weaknesses are in his supporting arguments.

Unfortunately, some students are not prepared to be challenged, and they confuse our questioning with personal criticism. Invariably, they have the educational process backward. Our job is not to reinforce their beliefs but to nurture their development as independent thinkers by pushing them to consider their—and others'—views. If my colleagues and I are doing our jobs right, we'll challenge the liberal students to consider the assumptions behind their arguments, question the conservative students about why they think as they do, and push the undecided and perplexed to work through their confusion to figure out what they think and can defend. We're not looking for students to be certain, have all the answers, or see the world in black and white. The mark of an educated person is the ability to recognize gray, appreciate nuance, and know the difference between a blustering assertion and a defensible position.

I know it may sound counterintuitive, but you really *do* want to take a class in which you get pushed to analyze the material and consider new ideas. The best courses move you outside your "comfort zone" and teach you how to think and become a critical consumer of information. At a minimum, you won't be bored in a class like this, and believe me, there are plenty of boring classes in college, the kind in which you'll be tempted to spend the semester texting your friends. If you want class to speed by, if you want to feel like the course has been worth your time and your money, then you need to elect a course that requires you to stretch yourself intellectually.

More importantly, classes like this are freeing. Being allowed to ask the "why" or "so what" questions is much more liberating than being expected to memorize facts. You'll rarely get this kind of intellectual freedom again—the freedom to consider the significance of a subject, to decide whether it matters and, if so, why. This is true no matter the subject. Consider an introductory class in a foreign language. Sure, much of the class will be taken up memorizing vocabulary and grammar, but that's not what will get you out of bed for an 8:00 a.m. class. Instead, it will be the professor who helps you to appreciate how the language holds together, who encourages you to try to communicate in an unusual dialect even if you don't know all the words, who inspires you to keep up with the subject. Too many students don't understand this imperative. They seek out the easy courses and then complain when they're bored or learn little.

The best classes are also fun. By that, I mean all involved—the professor and the students—look forward to coming to class. Surprisingly, this is not always related to the subject matter. How many of you would consider tax law to be fascinating? My guess is hardly any—including me for much of my life. But tax was my favorite class in law school, because I had a professor who went beyond the various parts of the tax code to explain to us why particular sections were created, what their effects had been, and how they all fit together. He was enthusiastic about his subject and encouraged us to consider the course as a giant jigsaw puzzle that we were putting together over the length of the term. No matter what subject you study, this is the kind of class you want to take, one in which the professor brings the subject alive even to the nonspecialist.

If it sounds like I'm pushing professor over subject matter, you're right. A really good instructor can teach anything he knows, and a student is much more likely to enjoy a class in which the instructor is good than a course whose subject matter initially seems interesting. Ask any college graduates you know what their favorite classes were and then ask why. Invariably, they'll describe the professor, and you'll likely hear the same qualities used to describe the instructor: a friendly soul who was interested in her subject, who challenged students to do their best, who was fair and prompt in returning assignments, and who, with a little luck, was funny as well as inspiring.

Teaching Assistants and Adjunct Instructors

You will notice that I'm talking about college faculty as if we're a uniform group. What I am describing is the great mass of full-time professors—tenured or tenure track—who regularly teach undergraduates. But we're not ubiquitous. At some schools, particularly at large universities, famous researchers rarely teach undergraduates and almost never appear in introductory classes for freshmen or sophomores. A few schools are beginning to challenge this pattern as their leaders recognize the importance of exposing entering students to the "big names" at the school. Not only does the interaction introduce students to the possibilities that await them should then delve deeper into a subject, but it also reminds senior faculty that, ultimately, the goal of research is to advance knowledge and improve conditions for the general public as well. If they cannot explain the intricacies of a subject to entering students, they run the risk of becoming caught so deep inside their specialty that they cannot recognize its overall relevance.

And there is an issue of fairness. It is the rare faculty member who looks forward to teaching classes of two hundred undergraduates. Frankly, most of us long for the fifteen-student seminar, the kind of class in which you get to know each student's thinking and can give him or her the kind of personal attention that helps to advance individual understanding. But the finances of modern colleges do not permit a plethora of small classes—at least not at research universities—so the duty of teaching large sections needs to be distributed. It is true that top researchers can often "buy out" their teaching by bringing in research grants. But still, each faculty member must teach some number of classes each year.

To cover a full complement of undergraduate classes with a faculty that is sometimes busy with funded research projects, most large universities employ teaching assistants or nontenured instructors to teach some classes. You may have heard of this practice before, which some critics decry as the "scandal" of university instruction. The argument goes like this: you have paid a lot of money to attend X University. X University lists a number of famous professors on its faculty, but few of these faculty members ever teach the classes you will take. It's a fraud, critics say, false advertising.

I do not doubt that universities could do a better job of explaining faculty loads, and at research-heavy institutions the teaching duties may border on false advertising. But this is different from fraud. Rather, it's a failure of many outside of academe (and several within) to understand the role of faculty members at most universities. If we are expected to conduct research and publish those findings—if, in fact, a college's bottom line depends upon us bringing in research funds—then we're not going to be available every semester to offer a full range of classes. To cover those courses, colleges increasingly have turned to graduate teaching assistants or temporary instructors.

TAs

Should you be worried if you sign up for a class only to find that your instructor is not a full-time professor? Usually not, although it depends to some extent on the subject. If the class is a large introductory course, it is not uncommon for a well-known professor to teach a large lecture hall and then have a graduate teaching assistant run an accompanying small discussion section. This exposes you to the professor for the primary course material and then allows you to meet with an auxiliary instructor who will answer questions and help you to apply the concepts from lecture. Most of the graduate students who facilitate these sections are advanced scholars in their fields and not only know the material well but also are sometimes more approachable, because they are closer in age to their undergraduate students. If you are in a class like this, don't worry: you're getting your money's worth.

Term Professors

Similarly, you'll be all right if you have a non–tenure-track professor who is experienced. Some universities employ these faculty members to teach the multitude of undergraduate classes, because the permanent faculty are consumed with research projects. The position *is* scandalous, but only in the way that these "term professors" are treated by their schools. Term faculty are expected to teach many more classes and are usually paid substantially less than are tenure-line faculty, despite the fact that most term faculty members have PhDs or similar academic qualifications. For a variety of reasons—including bad luck, geographic restrictions, or disinterest in research—term professors have not found tenure-line positions, so they accept jobs that give them more teaching responsibilities and fewer advantages than the permanent faculty has. It's a bit like sending the work of teaching undergraduates offshore to lower-paid employees. Is this scandalous when you're dealing with a computer company and your call gets routed to India to talk to a customer service? Apparently not, the business world thinks; but at universities the practice is considered more of a problem.

The good news for you is that most term professors are dedicated instructors and sometimes are even better teachers than the big-name professors, because they are expected to concentrate on teaching. Your concern should be the qualifications of the instructor. Is this someone who is actually trained in the subject she is teaching? How well does he know the literature in the field? Will he push you to engage with the material or only memorize facts? In some cases, how good is her English? These are a lot of questions for a student to consider, and I agree that it is fundamentally unfair that you should have to do this. But in these days of bottom-line education you need to be an informed consumer of your own education.

Adjuncts

The other instructor that may concern you is the temporary adjunct who is hired to teach a single class. Oftentimes, these instructors are professionals with expertise in a subject who are brought to campus for a semester to provide a broader perspective about a subject. This could be the local journalist who teaches a class about press and politics or the prosecutor who offers a course about constitutional procedure. The potential advantages in these classes are great: you may get to meet an interesting person you would not otherwise encounter, someone who can help you make sense of the distinction between academic theory and practical application. But it is also possible that these instructors will run a jumbled class, one in which an inexperienced teacher lurches from subject to subject, losing the students along the way. "Stories with Maury," the dig at classes in which a famous professional simply spins yarns rather than imparting knowledge, may sound like an easy and potentially interesting way to pass a semester, but you do not want to fill up an academic career with courses like these. They almost uniformly dispense facts rather than helping you to synthesize the subject's meaning or understand its importance.

What you're looking for in an adjunct or a term professor is the same thing you should be seeking in a permanent professor. Does this person know his field? Will she go beyond descriptions of "the way things are" to ask *why* things operate as they do or consider *whether* things should be done differently? Will he push you to critically assess ideas rather than accumulate and regurgitate information? Will she encourage you to do your best work? Can he explain complex concepts easily, and is he open to questions? Are you confident you will have learned new things by the end of the term? If you are satisfied with the answers to these questions, then, by all means take a course from one of these instructors.

Full-Time Faculty

That said, make sure that you seek out the full-time faculty for your other classes. Not only do we possess an institutional history of your school, but our mission is to connect research with teaching so that students understand and can converse on the latest findings in our fields. Most of us are good teachers as well, having become so if only by experience. I am still surprised to find some students who have gone the majority of their undergraduate careers without taking a class from a permanent faculty member. When I come across a student like this, it's usually someone who is piecing a degree together from night classes (which are more likely to be taught by adjuncts). But these students are losing out on important facets of a college education. For starters, they're more likely to be taught by instructors who may dispense facts in place of encouraging critical assessment. What's more, they're missing the chance to develop rapport with a professor who they might take for additional classes, a teacher who can help to nurture their intellectual (and sometimes personal) development, and who will be ready when their degrees are awarded to serve as a reference.

If there is one lesson in all of this, it is that you must take responsibility to vet the quality of your instructors when choosing classes. Unfortunately, you cannot rely on your school to ensure that the person teaching the class will be a top instructor. In truth, with their emphasis on research, universities don't always do this. But with the new economics at many schools—with incentives to hire lower-priced term professors who may lack a long-term commitment to the institution or even adjuncts who may be inexperienced in academe—you may be facing a catalog full of instructors who lack the backgrounds of your other professors and about whom there may be little information on their teaching. There is no need to panic; you can still get a great education. But it's up to you to identify the great teachers, the instructors who will expand your minds and make learning fun. You've undoubtedly heard the expression *caveat emptor,* let the buyer beware. When signing up for classes, that means you.

How to Identify Good Teachers

So how do you identify these top instructors? Fortunately, there are several sources. You should start with student teaching evaluations. Almost every college surveys its students each term, asking them to rate the quality of instruction in their classes. The results are then made available to successive waves of students. Don't make your judgment on a single semester—everyone can have an off class—but look for a professor who consistently scores high marks. You should also scan your college's website for past recipients of the school's teaching prize.

Depending upon your institution, this award is handed out annually to the professor, or group of professors, who are assessed by their colleagues to be top teachers. You will rarely go wrong with a professor who has won such an award, as the best teachers don't "phone it in" after winning.

I know some students scan RateMyProfessors.com for teacher assessments, but in most cases, the limited number of responses makes the evaluations unreliable. Better than this, go right to the source. Talk to a student who recently had the professor you are considering. Go sit in on a class the instructor is currently teaching to see what you think. Download a copy of a past syllabus from the class. Or even visit the professor during her office hours and talk to her directly about the class. Students rarely do this, but they really should. With annual tuition running as high as $40,000 at some colleges, the average class could cost as much as $5,000 per term. If you were buying a used car for that price you would take it out for a test drive first. Why not do the same for your classes?

Don't choose your class by the professor's grading scale, though. Once you get to campus, you'll undoubtedly hear about the professors who teach easy courses. In these classes almost everyone can earn an A if they show up and do a minimal amount of work. Of course, your GPA matters, especially if you aim for graduate school, but those easy classes are often the least interesting. Sure, you can sit in class content in the knowledge that your GPA won't suffer, but you're also likely to be bored. Boredom is the death knell of a college education.

There is an analogy here to the movies. Imagine that you're given a free pass to a new film, but when the lights go down and the movie fills the screen you find it simplistic, full of blather, and about as interesting as a dinner with your old Aunt Edna. Now imagine a movie that you've had to pay top dollar to screen. But it grabs you from the first image, expands your world, and makes you think about a provocative issue. In which theater would you prefer to spend your time? Sure, movies don't require the same amount of intellectual work that a class does, but ultimately you're agreeing to spend about 10 percent of the work week with each professor who teaches you. Multiply that by four classes and ask yourself whether you're prepared to be bored for that much of each week.

There are exceptions to this advice. Many seminars have high GPAs, often because these classes are reserved for honors students or departmental majors who are taking the "capstone" class in the field. In those classes, everyone is going to work hard and perform at their best, so it's not unusual to see high GPAs for these courses. From the other end, a class that consistently has a low GPA warrants caution, but here it's important to distinguish between professors who consistently grade lower than their peers and courses that are more difficult than others. The classic example of the latter is organic chemistry, a course that is sometimes used to "weed out" students considering medical school. Most sections of this class have lower GPAs than do other classes in a school's chemistry department regardless of the instructor. Sometimes you'll want to take a class with a low GPA *because* the professor is a tough grader. Excelling in a class like that can be a badge of honor—whether at your school where the professor is well known or sometimes at graduate schools where his reputation precedes him. Tough graders almost always are sticklers for standards and push their students to perform at their highest level. Take a class like this and you'll be challenging yourself to see where you measure up.

Getting the Most from Faculty

You should begin each course with the goal of staying on a professor's good side. Not because we're going to penalize you if we don't like you. Your grade, after all, will be a measure of what you accomplish in the course, not a stand-in for what we think of you personally. Rather, what you want from the professor is his attention, his willingness to explain subjects a different way if you're having difficulty understanding them at first, his interest in your intellectual and personal development, and ultimately his recommendation if you go on for further study or need a reference for a job.

Attend Class

Professors, actually, are fairly uncomplicated. There are five keys to earning our interest and attention. First, always show up to class. You'll be lost if you don't, but more instrumentally, we will quickly learn to identify you as the student who doesn't care enough to even show up, and that is not the kind of attention you want to draw to yourself. It is a disservice to you and to us.

Be Prepared

It is not enough simply to attend class; you also need to come prepared. Do the assigned reading. Complete any written assignments. Stay on top of the material. Passive learning is nowhere near as effective as a classroom of responsible and involved students. So do your prep work. There is no quicker way to disrespect a teacher than coming to class having ignored the reading. You might as well say, "I have no interest in what you're trying to accomplish here." A reputation can be quickly earned, and you do not want to spend most of the semester trying to live down an impression that you're unengaged and disinterested.

Participate Regularly

Participate in class discussions but don't seek to dominate the exchange. This is a difficult piece of advice, I recognize. Some students are shyer than others, and the bashful may be reluctant to speak up. But keep in mind that your professors will have little sense of your thinking, your temperament, or your style unless you speak up from time to time. Even if it's just to answer a question with an obvious response, chime in so that we recognize your voice. Besides, it's inevitably the wallflowers who add an important perspective to class discussion when they do join the conversation.

If you're hesitant to speak in a large class, wait until the professor breaks the class into smaller groups for a project and then join in. But please resist the urge to raise your hand at every turn or talk just to hear your own voice. We all know these students; they can often be found in the first two rows of class with their hands perpetually in the air. Although faculty may depend on them to keep class discussion rolling when others are silent, we're trying to involve the whole class in the exercise. So don't be surprised if we seem to ignore your outstretched arm to call on someone else to join the conversation.

Confess Your Confusion

Let us see your struggle; it tells us that you're learning. If you're trying to get your brain around a concept in class, stop us and explain where you're confused. We'll try to teach the concept a different way. If you think you're missing a prerequisite that the rest of the class seems to have, let us know so we can steer you to the appropriate resources. If the class is just plain hard for you but you're willing to put in the effort, come talk to us about how we might help you in other ways. Or, if a subject really interests you and you want to explore it in greater detail, let us know. We'll be delighted to point you to additional sources or opportunities.

Utilize Office Hours

Come talk to us, whether after class or during office hours. Unlike high school teachers, college professors are required to keep several hours open each week in which students can come talk to them. We're available to expand upon class discussion, help students prepare for exams, offer advice about graduate school or job opportunities, or just talk about politics, sports, or life in general. But with the exception of some liberal arts colleges, far too few students take advantage of this opportunity. It's mystifying. If you're one of 250 students in a class at a large state school, you may never see the professor up close in class. But if you come to office hours you can receive personal instruction, get your questions answered, and receive hints on studying for the course.

Think of office hours as advanced tutoring, an opportunity to leverage your tuition for the kind of one-on-one dialogue depicted in promotional literature but harder to achieve in practice. It is the rare instructor who does not admire students with the dedication to come to office hours with questions about the class material or their academic plans. You may also develop a professional friendship with the professor, who is then in a better position to provide you a reference later on. As I explain in my classes, I will not write letters of recommendation for students I barely know. Having sat on enough graduate admissions committees, I know these letters are unhelpful. The references that make a difference are those in which the professor can write meaningfully and at length about the student's strengths, interests, and goals. That information is only available if the student has made a point of getting to know the professor through the years, which generally requires an effort more than just showing up in class.

Of course, it can sometimes be a fine line between mentoring and groupie status, so recognize the limits of a professional friendship by sharing office hours with your classmates. Don't call your professor at home or text him at night unless the syllabus distinctly allows it. Personal space can be a difficult concept for certain students to understand when they're used to displaying their most private thoughts on their

Facebook pages, but professors—who are still of an earlier generation—expect a zone of privacy for their personal lives. Better to use e-mail to contact your professor so she can answer you quickly but at a time that does not intrude on her personal life.

Ultimately, what you're looking for with your professors is a professional relationship of mutual respect, one in which you take an active responsibility for your education by coming to class prepared, meeting deadlines, and asking lots of questions when you're curious or confused. In return, you should expect your professors to seek to engage you, challenge you, nurture your development as a scholar and as a person, and give of their time to further your education. That is the depiction of college often found in movies and books, and it is one still available at many colleges—if you look for it and take an active role in its development. In many ways, however, the responsibility is yours.

2

. . . .

FINDING THE BEST CLASSES
AND CHOOSING THE RIGHT
MAJOR

How to Decide What to Study

At most colleges you are likely to face a series of "core" course requirements as a first-year student. Sometimes called general education requirements, these classes are designed to give you a broad familiarity with the essential "anchors" of American education. You'll likely have to take a class in English composition, perhaps another in literature, a course in math or analytical reasoning, maybe a few in a foreign language, and several chosen from among the various fields in humanities, natural sciences, and social sciences. Schools vary in the amount of flexibility they grant students when selecting their core classes. I have taught at colleges that mandate a series of sixteen classes in the first two years and others that provide significant latitude so long as students show some diversity in their course selection.

The core curriculum tries to balance two competing tensions in a college education. Unlike high school, in college *you* get to choose what you want to study. You don't have any interest in German? No problem; no one is going to force you to learn it. You love art history? Great, you'll be able to take courses in the subject. But at the same time, we want to make sure you're well rounded, that an education in one field does not come at the expense of learning something about a wider range of subjects. Consider for a moment just how many more fields of study there are at college than in high school. Even the most modest of small colleges offer classes in such diverse areas as sociology, economics, anthropology, philosophy, Spanish, geology, and psychology, just to name a few. At larger schools you'll find courses in Arabic, Japanese literature, biochemistry, accounting, music appreciation, and thousands of other unusual subjects. Even the most resource-intensive high schools cannot compete with the diversity and depth of subjects offered at college.

So before we lose you to the specialization of your major, we want to make sure that you have the basic building blocks of an informed citizen. This is the basis of the liberal arts, a term that refers to the breadth of a college education rather than the political ideology of the campus you'll attend. Even a student of animal husbandry needs to know how to express herself in written or oral communication. Computer scientists will understand their foreign colleagues better if they have had a class in comparative culture. A marketing manager may relate better to his customers if he has studied psychology. Even lawyers may appreciate the logic that comes with math and music composition.

The point of the liberal arts is that education has its own intrinsic value, that an educated person should seek to be curious about the world around her and wish to learn simply because it will make her a more knowledgeable and interesting person. There are hundreds of small colleges around the country dedicated to this very principle. Schools from Amherst to Beloit, Colgate to Dennison, Earlham, Franklin and Marshall to Goucher and Haverford—we could almost name the alphabet with the range of liberal arts institutions in the U.S. But even junior colleges and preprofessional university programs recognize the value of a broad base of coursework on which to build one's specialization.

Study What Interests *You*

Most high school students contemplating college will undoubtedly encounter friends, relatives, and even teachers who purport to advise them on their college coursework. It's like a scene in the classic movie, *The Graduate*, where a businessman advises a young Dustin Hoffman on a career. Turning to the younger man at a cocktail party, he barks out, "One word—plastics," to a bewildered Hoffman. Today, that same businessman might encourage Hoffman to study computers, Chinese, or even genetics. But the truth of the matter is that, apart from those core classes, you should study what interests you.

This concept, so basic and true, may seem novel to some students. Throughout high school, many of them have been told what they must study, whether by the state board of education that mandates the curriculum or by their parents and high school counselors who insist on particular classes to make their applications "competitive" for college admissions. Other students are advised to the point of hounding by their parents to study a "practical subject" that will help them get a job when they graduate. Then suddenly they show up at orientation and confront the large catalog of classes only to be paralyzed by indecision.

I once was one of these students. Encouraged to follow a "college-bound" curriculum in high school, I took "the basics" in school—English, math, science, and a foreign language. I avoided elective classes like journalism, which I would have loved, because they weren't part of the prescribed path to college. Then I arrived on the campus of a large university with a menu of classes that went on for pages. Could I take a risk on some of these classes, I asked myself. Would they put me on that mythical path to "success?" My parents were paying a hefty price for me to be there. How would they feel if I took classes in social psychology or gender studies, subjects not usually associated with a lucrative career?

What I quickly came to realize as a student—and now know to be true as a professor—is that no one can command your interests. Some of us find electronics fascinating, others cannot imagine anything duller. Philosophy strikes a chord with one group, another considers it impossible to follow. I have taught political science and law; some of my relatives do not share my interest in the subjects, just as I have little interest (or ability) in graphic art.

As a college student, the upshot of this lesson is that you should study what interests you. Not what interests your parents. Not what your relatives or parents' friends advise. Not what your friends tell you. Not even what you think employers want you to study. In the end, you will find the most enjoyment and do your best work in what appeals to you, and you will eventually find your way professionally in those fields that grab you and where you have excelled.

It's Okay to Not Know

Maybe you don't know yet what interests you. That's fine. Most entering college students are just eighteen years old. The notion that you should know now what you want to do with "the rest of your life" not only is unrealistic but also puts too much pressure on you to plan out your life. There are few decisions at this age that cannot be reversed, excursions into potential interests that cannot stand a detour or two. One of the central advantages of college is the opportunity to figure out who and what you are. This is a time to experiment, to reinvent yourself over and over again if need be. No matter who is paying for college—and I realize most students owe an enormous debt to their parents for footing the bill—it's you who needs to emerge intact at the end of the four (or more) years, happy with who you have become. Did you play it safe, afraid of testing the limits of your interests, or did you give yourself the freedom to follow a path that grabs you?

No matter why you've decided on college—whether to learn more things, to pursue a definite field, to find a good job, or just to get away from home for a few years—you are wasting a precious opportunity if you don't allow yourself the opportunity to venture outside of your comfort zone. Take a class in something you've never heard of before; try to understand the perspective of someone with whom you disagree; travel to a foreign country where you're unfamiliar with the culture. You will grow in the process, becoming the kind of person you would respect if you happened to meet this stranger on the street.

I know it sounds like I'm preaching, but it's because I cannot emphasize this point enough: too many college students are chicken. They're being raised in hermetically sealed environments by overprotective parents who don't allow them the chance to fall off course from the assumed and singular path to "success." You've already made it to college. Now it's *your* turn to craft your own life and life experiences. It's time to follow your own interests for no other reason than it's your life. Success, I promise, will find you if you're passionate about what you do, if you develop the skills to follow those interests after college. And let's not forget that success has many forms. If you're lucky, the friends you meet at college and the professors who teach you there will remain friends and mentors for decades to come. Throw yourself into the opportunity. One of the reasons college is so expensive is because of the opportunities it affords in so many areas of your life. Don't chicken out.

Choosing Classes

Okay, you say, this is all very nice in theory. You're ready to give it the old college try, but how do you figure out what interests you? You're looking at a giant course catalog with lots of possibilities. What should you take at college?

Start with the most obvious classes—those you are required to take. Some of these may be part of the core requirements mentioned above, and others are prerequisites to take upper-level classes in a subject. The most obvious example of the latter is an introductory class in a foreign language. It goes without saying that you cannot read French literature until you first understand its grammar and vocabulary. Similarly, most fields have introductory courses that students must take before continuing in the discipline. So if you have an inkling that a course in group psychology might interest you, be sure to take the introductory class in psychology early in your college career. If you're interested in capital markets, make sure you take the prerequisite class in introductory economics.

You will be able to identify introductory classes in two ways. The majority are listed as prerequisites in upper-level course listings. So if you continually see Political Science 100 listed as the prerequisite for upper-level classes, you will know that course is the introductory class. Beginning classes also have numerical identifiers that begin with a 1, like Math 101, Psychology 110, or Biology 100. Most colleges use a three-digit formula for identifying classes. Courses designed for freshmen and sophomores begin with a 1 or 2, and those intended for upper-level students start with a 3 or 4.

The rest of a course's identification number is simply its unique code. A few schools use two-digit numbers for their classes—say, English 10—but, again, freshmen and sophomores would generally take classes that begin with a 1 or 2, and juniors and seniors would take classes that start with a 3 or 4. This does not mean that upper-level students are barred from taking classes at the 100 or 200 level. In fact, many college juniors and seniors will elect introductory classes in other areas, whether to satisfy distribution requirements, try out a subject that has always interested them, or change their majors entirely. But the reverse is not true. Unless a student has been excused from the course prerequisites—either because she has advanced credit in the subject or is just familiar with the material—it would be foolish to begin with an upper-level class. The analogy here is jumping into the deep end of a pool without first knowing how to swim. Get your feet wet, learn how to maneuver in the medium, and then dive into the deep stuff.

What Is a Major and When Should You Choose One?

Eventually, almost every college will require you to choose a major. Think of a major as your specialty, the field in which you will take at least the plurality of your courses. At a school that requires 120 course credits in order to graduate, upwards of 60 or 75 of those will likely be in your major. This is not as onerous as it may sound, since many of those credits are actually prerequisites or cognates found in other departments. Choose to major in biology, for example, and you'll likely have to take courses in chemistry, too. Concentrate in American politics, and you will need courses in U.S. history, as well.

There is no need to choose a major until your junior year, so don't fall victim to the fallacy that you need to know on day one what specialty interests you. Many students change their majors two or three times in their first years at college as they explore the many options available. But by the time you reach the start of your third year at school you should be in the process of winnowing the options so you can spend your final two years completing the requirements for your major.

You may have heard that some students now take five or more years to finish college. Some news stories place the blame on overcrowded classes that students need but cannot select for their major, so don't wait until the last minute to choose a major. From my own observations, it's usually the students who suddenly decide to change their major in their senior year who stick around for an extra semester or two. Mind you, this is not the end of the world, and if you find your interests changing, then by all means consider classes in a new field. But if your goal is to be in and out of college in four years, then file your choice of major by the start of your junior year and keep a checklist of the courses you will need to complete to be cleared to graduate. Depending upon your school, an academic advisor may be assigned to help you keep track of these requirements, but ultimately the responsibility is yours.

There Are Not Magic Majors

The process of choosing a major is virtually the same as determining which classes to take as a freshmen or sophomore: go with what interests you. Unless you're sure you want to be an accountant or nurse—two professions that require specific majors—there is no need to select a major with a particular career in mind. In truth, the value of most college educations is the disciplined reasoning and sophisticated communication skills you will pick up while studying, not whether you specialized in English or botany. To be sure, you can show a future employer that you are interested in her field by the courses you took in college, but the point is kind of a tautology: you're unlikely to pursue a career in a field that does not interest you, just as you will not major in an area you find boring.

This is a point that many students—and especially their parents—often find difficult to accept. Especially among first-generation college attendees, the pressure to study something "practical" is intense. "Study engineering, computers, or economics," many a parent has told his college-age child, "because that is where the jobs are." True, there are often entry-level jobs available in the high-tech world, but by no means do businesses in these fields hire only students who majored in these areas. For that matter, there are many companies and organizations in other fields that are looking for well-rounded students, college graduates whose most attractive quality is their ability to think creatively and find new solutions to pressing problems.

This advice is all the more true for students who wish to go on to professional schools, mainly law, medical, and veterinary programs. In fact, let's take a little quiz. Can you name the majors with the highest acceptance rates into these programs? If you're like many people, you probably said political science for law and biology or chemistry for medical and veterinary schools. Certainly, students from these majors often go on to the related professional schools, but none of these majors has the highest acceptance rate. In fact, a study of applicants to medical school found that an applicant's major had no bearing on his or her acceptance, and studies of law school admissions routinely find that diverse majors such as music, math, and physics have the highest acceptance rates for legal study.

To be sure, professional schools often demand certain course prerequisites. Medical schools, for example, will not accept applicants who have failed to take at least one course in biology, physics, and organic and inorganic chemistry. But these are four classes out of a full undergraduate career. There is absolutely no reason to take a "pre-law" or "pre-med" major if you want to pursue a different field during your undergraduate days before specializing in professional school. What graduate programs seek from applicants—and I know because I have sat on their admissions committees—are three things: high test scores from the admissions exams, strong letters of recommendation from professors with whom students have worked closely, and good grades in classes that challenged students to think critically and express themselves clearly. For now, don't worry about those entrance exams (more on those in chapter 6). What you can control is the academic program you take and the professional relationships you strike up with your instructors. There is *not* a magic major for professional success. Choose a major that interests you and one in which you will be motivated to work hard.

Alternative Majors, Double Majors, and Minors

If you're one of those students who finds the notion of a major too limiting, some schools have concentrations in general studies. Contrary to their name, many of these majors do not require you to concentrate at all. You can take a variety of classes from across several disciplines and piece them together into a coherent whole that serves your interests. The same is true for independent concentrations, a path I pursued in college. My alma mater did not have an undergraduate program in public policy, so with a professor's oversight I created an independent major with courses from political science, economics, history, sociology, and statistics.

For those students with multiple interests, there is also the option of majoring in more than one subject—a practice known as a double major—or even the possibility of electing a minor in addition to a major. Most majors track the names of your school's academic departments. The sociology department, for example, sponsors a sociology major. Some interdisciplinary subjects, however, are shared between a couple of departments. Often known as minors, these fields permit students to supplement their specialized study with coursework in a cross- or sub-disciplinary field. Philosophy and law is a classic example of a minor. Some departments even offer miniaturized versions of their majors as minors. So if you're stuck trying to choose between two fields, you may decide to major in one area and minor in the other. Your concentrations should be a reflection of your interests, not the other way around.

Determining Your Interests

You may have noted a theme by now in this chapter—a strong recommendation to pursue those classes and those fields that interest you. It's well known, however, that a free choice can be stressful to some people, especially those who have been used to relying on others—say, teachers, guidance counselors, and parents—to tell them what subjects to study over the years. Remind you of anyone you know? How do you figure this question out for yourself? There are five essential principles.

First, select broadly from a variety of classes in your first few years. If nothing else, you will learn what does not interest you. Strange as it may sound, that is an essential part of the winnowing process. Second, go to a variety of talks on campus. Most departments host visiting speakers throughout the academic year. If an event sounds mildly interesting and you have the time, go sit in for a bit to see what questions are being debated in various disciplines. Even if you merely rule out a possible major, this is progress, although you're just as likely to find a kernel of interest in the fields you go explore.

Third, get involved with extracurricular activities on campus. The key is to try new things, to open yourself up to experiences that may strike a chord in you. You would be amazed by how many nurses or social workers first found their calling by volunteering with troubled youth or in a hospital emergency room while at college.

Fourth, consider talking to professors you have liked or speak with an academic advisor. At some colleges, faculty serve as academic advisors, available to help students plan their schedules and consider academic alternatives. At other schools, there are dedicated staff to advise students on classes. Either way, you should make a point of seeking out your school's advising resources as you think about majors. Academic advisors will be able to explain the prerequisites for various majors and minors and help to walk you through the process of planning out subsequent semesters so you can complete your degree in due time.

Finally, and this may be the most important principle of all, do not put added pressure on yourself. Do you remember when you first learned to ride a bike? Like most children, you had to fall over a few times before your body got the feel of balancing a two-wheeler. You couldn't will the learning process simply by declaring yourself a master of bike riding. You picked up the skill once you had practiced and your body got the hang of it.

Choosing a major is surprisingly similar. You're going to waver several times; some days you'll be interested in one field, another day you'll lurch in a different direction. It is the rare student who knows from the beginning exactly what she wants to study and, in fact, sometimes these students learn much later in life that they were only trying to convince themselves of an interest, because they were fearful of appearing indecisive. It is perfectly all right not to know what grabs you as you begin college, and you need to give yourself the license to explore your interests at your own pace.

As I often tell my students, do not make the mistake of comparing your inner to someone else's outer. At some point, you'll undoubtedly look at some of your classmates with envy, wishing that you felt as sure, knowing, and confident as they seem to be. But you don't know what they're telling themselves privately. In all likelihood, they're just as insecure and unsure as you are—they just won't admit it outwardly. So if nothing else, go easy on yourself in your expectations. Select from a variety of classes, challenge yourself where possible, and take responsibility for doing your best work as often as you can. These three keys will bring you both personal pride and a rewarding four years at college.

Prior Credit

It's not uncommon for students to arrive a college with advanced course credit. Some of these students take advanced placement classes in high school and score high enough on achievement tests to receive college credit. Other students may have studied at a community college before enrolling at a four-year institution. Either way, prior course credit opens up opportunities. In many cases, students bring credit for one or two classes. The classic example is the student who took AP English and U.S. history, earning six to eight credits in the process. Here, the prior credit will allow her to waive prerequisites in these subjects while giving her some flexibility not to take a full course load (or, at some schools, pay full tuition) for one semester while still graduating on schedule.

In other cases, students may bring one or more semester's worth of credit. If this is the case, students may have the opportunity to graduate early, thereby saving themselves and their families valuable tuition dollars. In some cases, students with a semester's worth of prior credit will decide to take classes during the summer in order to speed up the process and graduate in the spring after three academic years on campus.

I have mixed feelings about speeding up college. On one hand, I am well aware that many colleges are expensive to attend. On the other hand, I believe that the four years are a valuable resource that should not be rushed. There is so much to be gleaned from classes, extracurricular activities, friendships, and relationships. Sometimes I even want to take students aside and plead, "cherish this time while you have it. It's a gift that will keep on giving all of your life."

So if you are going to speed up your college years, whether by starting early through advanced placement classes or going to summer school to graduate faster, make sure you take full advantage of the opportunities that college offers. Try a subject you know nothing about, make friends with someone from a completely different background, find a mentor in a faculty member. Give yourself the time and opportunity to grow.

Distance Learning

If you have ever ridden a subway in an American city, you undoubtedly have been confronted with a poster for a "distance university," a college "without borders" that permits you to take classes online and earn your degree without the "inconvenience" of trying to schedule classes around your other activities. Their message may sound appealing. Is it even necessary to enroll in a brick-and-mortar school when there are several institutions—the University of Phoenix, Walden University, or Capella University, for example—that do not require on-site class attendance?

It depends to a large extent on what you seek to experience in college. If your desire is simply a credential, a college diploma, then an online school may be a good option for you. But keep in mind that the academic reputation of most of these schools is suspect, in part because many of them are for-profit companies and not traditional educational institutions.[1] If you enroll at a school like this you're essentially banking on the fact that your future employers won't know much about college reputations and will be satisfied with the fact that you have a college degree, no matter the institution. This may suffice in some professions, but the higher you climb up the ladder of professional prestige in America, the more likely it is that this strategy will not fly. Graduate and professional schools all know which undergraduate institutions require real work out of their students and which ones do not. Many employers, too, are looking for students who graduated from schools with which they are familiar, whether these be "brand name" institutions or local schools with decent reputations.

Even well-known schools are now offering some classes online, freeing students to take classes at their own pace while learning from a professor who appears in virtual time. I know of several good students who praise online education, but as a professor I need to warn you about them, for an online class cannot fully replicate what a professor provides for you in the classroom. True, an online class is effective at imparting information, and you will likely receive effective feedback on your written work. You may even engage in an interesting dialogue with your professor and classmates as people log in to respond to each other's comments on the course site. All of these are valuable, but the true value that any of my colleagues or I provide in the classroom is the chance to ask questions—and have them answered—as they occur to students, to push students to think on their feet, and to provide positive reinforcement that comes in louder and clearer when given face-to-face.

This is not the usual criticism of the Internet, that virtual enthusiasts discount the importance of human interaction. It's not just that there is value in sitting in a room with a group of people at one time hearing the lectures and student reactions in real time. It's also my ability to push students while they are still formulating an idea that causes them to consider their views more carefully. I can see what is confusing them and address their concerns immediately rather than waiting for them to notice the disjuncture in their thoughts as they are studying for an exam. I can create student debate and encourage classmates to think on their feet. This is a real life skill, one that really cannot be replicated by waiting for students to respond to a question in the Ethernet.

Skeptical? Okay, think of a television news show, say *Meet the Press* or some other program that pits newsmakers against journalists in a live discussion. Do you get something different—actually better—out of that format than if the reporters simply submitted their questions in writing and allowed the policymakers to respond? How interesting would you find it and how fast do you think the politicians would learn the skill of thinking cogently on their feet if they were given hours or even days before responding to follow-up questions? The situation is similar in distance learning. Sure, a professor can engage you with a question online, and you'll likely learn from the process of weighing the query and structuring your answer. (This is, after all, why we assign papers.) But there is a lot to be gained through the collective and immediate effort of questions, answers, and discussion that can be done while people face one another, reading each other's nonverbal communication, and addressing one another in person. I do not mean to swear you off from online classes completely; I would encourage you to use them sparingly. If there is a class you need and you just cannot fit it into your schedule, then, fine, think of taking it online. But if you're trying to make the most out of your college experience, take the vast majority of your classes in person.

Experiential Education

Another trend in collegiate education these days is experiential education. Experiential education appears generally in one of two formats. Some schools profess to offer students course credit for "life experience." Curiously, such schools also seem to be clustered among the for-profit, their owners essentially selling prospective students course credits for jobs or other work experience that students bring with them to college. It may sound attractive—hey, you can knock off degree requirements without having to take classes—but you should be careful that you are not choosing a college that provides little else for your money than a degree to hide among your papers. Admittedly, some "brand name" schools now offer up to fifteen credits for a student's portfolio of "prior learning," but these institutions follow standards set by the Council for Adult and Experiential Learning to ensure that credit is granted for work that "led to theoretical as well as practical knowledge."[2] Any school that offers you credit for generic "experience" is not worth attending.

Not all experiential education offerings are inferior. A number of schools are beginning to offer for undergraduates the kind of clinical courses that are common at law and medical schools. The concept is similar—providing opportunities for students to test theories and ideas from the classroom with practical experience, then bringing students back to the classroom to assess the interaction of the two. For some schools, experiential education means credit for student internships. At others, including a class I have taught, students are added to legal or campaign teams to observe and participate in high-stakes projects.

Rather than "pay for credit" schemes, these classes do not simply award students credit for their work. A good experiential education program has classroom components at the beginning and end of the internship or project so that students are led quite deliberately to consider their experiences at work against the academic theories that conceptualize these activities. Students are assigned readings in these classes and are required to complete regular "reflection" papers in which they size up the readings against their work on the ground. The courses typically end with a term paper in which students are asked to synthesize the lessons of the internship or experiential work.

If your school offers classes like this, don't worry about registering for them. As a supplement to an otherwise stimulating collection of classes, experiential education is a good alternative and, in some cases, a helpful transition from college life to career. I know of several students, in fact, who turned an internship into a job upon graduation and who today have fashioned interesting careers in fields that first intrigued them during an experiential education class.

Study Abroad

As a prospective student you may have heard about the possibility of studying abroad for a year. Many schools offer these programs, typically encouraging students in their junior year of college to spend a semester or academic year studying at a different institution. Previously the province of European locales, study-abroad programs now offer students the chance to spend time on each of the seven continents. Like experiential education programs, a year abroad gives you the opportunity to measure your college education—and your life experience— against the norms of another educational system and country.

Most study-abroad programs provide instruction in English but also may encourage students to participate in an "immersion program," in which they either take other classes in the language of the host country or reside with a local family who does not speak English. The point, of course, is to improve a student's ability in the foreign language while creating a cross-cultural experience.

Some study-abroad programs are more demanding than others. Certainly, there are those that require little of a student besides attending a few classes in the morning, allowing the visitor to "chill out" at local cafes the rest of the day. Some students even try to arrange all of their classes on Tuesdays through Thursdays so they can use the other four days of the week to travel throughout the countryside. There are other programs, however, that are so demanding that students rarely see sights off campus. In these courses students may be trying just to keep up with instruction offered in the local language.

No matter the study abroad program you select, there are distinct advantages to be had from spending a semester or year away from your comfort zone. Whether it is classroom learning, interacting with other students outside of class, or trying to navigate your way through a city (and culture) where you don't understand the language, you will likely grow significantly and learn considerably if you try some time abroad. For that matter, most colleges permit students to pay the same tuition rate while on a study-abroad program, so except for your travel expenses, the cost of studying in a foreign country may not wipe out your bank account.

How to Pick a Program

There are several key questions that you should ask yourself when considering a program. First, where do you want to study? There is no "right" answer here, because ultimately the choice is yours. Are you interested in exploring a classical civilization? Then France, Italy, Greece, or Turkey may be your best option. Do you want to investigate your family's heritage, perfect a language you are learning, or explore a developing country? The reasons for studying abroad are as plentiful as the number of programs offered.

Second, are you satisfied with the study-abroad options your school offers? It's almost always easier to study through your own school, if only because gaining credit for courses taken abroad is routine. If you're interested in a country not covered by your school, look around for programs offered by other colleges, but make sure to check with your own registrar's office ahead of time to confirm that the courses—and credits—will be accepted into your own program.

Third, how well do you know the language of the host country, and are you interested in learning it? As mentioned above, many study-abroad programs offer instruction in English, but this is not universal. Some emphasize mastering the local language, and others do not. Some foreign schools may even accept international visitors without offering a formal program for them. In this case, you may find yourself in over your head if you show up without a good command of the indigenous language and some knowledge of the local customs.

Finally, take a hard look at how difficult the courses are likely to be for you. If a program is offered by an American college and staffed by U.S. faculty, its classes and expectations are likely to be familiar to you, even if there is an immersion component in the local language. Keep in mind, again, that many of these programs are open to students from colleges across America, so they may have a tendency to target the abilities of the "average student." Programs offered directly from a foreign institution, however, may have different expectations and require greater effort of visiting students. So make sure you read the promotional literature carefully, surf the Internet for feedback, and ask to communicate with students who have participated in the programs before. A semester or year abroad can be a defining moment in a college career, but just as you were urged to do when learning to swim, look before you leap.

Other Opportunities

If a semester or year abroad is not for you, there are other ways of broadening your education. Many schools offer travel programs for credit in which students spend winter, spring, or summer break with a professor visiting a city or region and learning about the language or culture there. Laced with readings, discussions, and writing assignments, these shorter voyages can still earn students course credit and an eye-opening experience. A brief review of the offerings at several universities finds faculty-led study tours to Costa Rica, Ecuador, Egypt, Israel, Ireland, London, and Rome. On the Costa Rican trip, for example, students study biodiversity, ecology, and environmental preservation on-site in one of the most diverse rain forests in the world. We all know instinctively that the world is getting smaller, but sometimes it takes a firsthand experience to bring the lesson home. Study abroad, no matter how long the excursion, is another chance to broaden your horizons.

■

College offers you many opportunities for study, but don't let the choices paralyze you. Your initial task is to select classes that are interesting to you, that will challenge you, and that will help you to identify potential fields for further exploration. There will be plenty of time for specialization, so don't get caught up in the charade that you must choose a major quickly or succumb to the pressure to "figure out" your plans right away. College should be a period of intellectual freedom, of personal growth. If nothing else, give yourself the space to figure out what interests you so you can pursue your own path.

3

···

IN THE CLASSROOM

Okay, you've managed to sign up for classes, and, if you're wise, you already have mapped them out on campus so you know how to get from building to building. But before you set foot inside your first college class, you ought to be prepared for what to expect. For unlike high school classes that were likely taught in a uniform manner, college courses vary considerably.

If you were like most high school students, you were taught in classes of about twenty to thirty students by a teacher who alternately employed lecture and discussion. You likely knew the names of most of your classmates and probably even recognized their voices since your teachers would call on students from time to time to participate in class discussion or at least answer a question. Classes met every day for the same amount of time in rooms that closely resembled one another.

In college, this description would not cover a single class, since courses are offered in many forms. In general, though, you're most likely to see three forms of instruction: lecture, lecture with discussion sections, and seminars. Depending on the subject, classes may meet for as little as one two-hour session each week or as often as four days per week for a total of five hours. Lecture classes are just what they sound like and are found most likely in introductory or prerequisite courses. At large public universities it is not unusual to find yourself in a lecture hall with two hundred other students for History 101 while you squint to see the professor several rows ahead at a podium with a portable microphone. I know of courses taught to six hundred students, some of them even sitting in auxiliary classrooms watching the professor on a closed-circuit screen. At one school, the enrollment for a required introductory course was so great that the professor taped all of his lectures and had them played on the university's cable station.

Fortunately, these classes are rare—and they should be. They envision education as exclusively one-way: students are seen as empty vessels to be filled with "knowledge" simply through a professor's grand pronouncements. Yet virtually all of the research on teaching shows that effective instruction is interactive, drawing students into the subject and encouraging them to question and employ the ideas being presented. The same research suggests that it's useful for the instructor to switch gears every twenty to thirty minutes to keep students' attention. If a professor spends time lecturing about basic terms, she needs to stop and employ an exercise for students to apply those terms. If she shows a movie, she needs to stop it from time to time for students to ask questions. Some of this should be intuitive: no one wants to be bored, and bored minds are ineffective learners.

Surviving Large Classes

If you find yourself in a large lecture class, you have to hope that the professor is at least entertaining. A friend of mine is quite candid about his job in teaching introductory lecture courses. "I'm an entertainer," he says, "not a teacher." He explains, "When you look out at a class of three hundred students, you know that you're not going to be able to reach each of them individually. So your best bet is to try to keep their interest up so that they'll want to learn the material." Sharing stories and telling jokes are techniques any professor may use to lighten a classroom atmosphere, but they are more crucial in a large lecture where the focus of all of those students' eyes is on the professor, who is charged with keeping their attention and not losing command of the classroom.

Ever since I was an undergraduate, I have disliked large lecture classes, although my reasons have changed over the years. Initially, I felt disrespected by the university, which I thought was playing me and my family for fools; there I was, one of two hundred students in a large lecture hall, paying good money to listen to some "great mind" speak at me for fifty minutes a day. Now, as a professor, I dislike these classes because I don't think students learn as much in them. Sure, the best students will be able to recite back the information that was imparted over the length of the semester. But will they understand why those topics are so important, how they can be applied, and what their limits may be? Not as well as if the students were encouraged to ask questions during class or were challenged to work through the concepts with in-class exercises. That's why I refuse to treat large classes as one-way lecture series. Even in a course of two hundred students, I've been known to teach as if the class had only twenty-five. I'll roam around the room, encouraging students to take a stand on an issue and then encourage debates. I'll break up the room into small groups to discuss an issue and then report their findings back to the whole class. I also keep a big bowl of candy at the front of the room, which I'll share with volunteers who agree to participate in role-playing exercises. Invariably, the students enjoy these classes better than a one-way lecture, as do I.

Lecture-Discussion Classes

I'm not saying that I've patented some magic formula for effective teaching, but there is a lesson here for you: wherever possible, steer away from classes that envision you as sheep, passively sitting in a large classroom being lectured at while you copy down the "lessons" being imparted. Most colleges know this as well, which is why many lecture courses are paired with smaller discussion sections. The idea is that you attend a large lecture two or three times per week and then participate in a smaller section of ten to twenty-five students for an additional session once a week. If in the large lectures you're expected to listen and take notes, in the discussion sections the instructor will be available to answer questions about the material, engage you in discussion about the finer details of the subject, and help you to apply the ideas with different exercises.

The only catch is that discussion sections are rarely led by the professor. Instead, most colleges employ graduate students or adjunct instructors to facilitate these sessions. That is not necessarily a bad thing, since discussion sections are usually employed in introductory classes and graduate students are closer to remembering what it was like to approach the material from the start. But if you're looking for a course in which you will get personal instruction from a veteran faculty member, lecture courses are not a good bet. There is one exception, though. As you look through the time schedule, you may see a course in which the instructor listed for the lecture portion of the course also is scheduled next to a few discussion sections. This is a sign that the professor plans to share responsibility for the discussion sections So if you were to sign up for one of his discussion sections not only you would hear the professor's lectures in class, you also would get more individual attention in discussion.

Seminars

The descriptions above apply almost exclusively to large research universities—schools such as the University of Wisconsin, the University at Albany, and Arizona State University. Smaller schools, and especially liberal arts colleges, try to avoid large lecture classes. These schools typically emphasize teaching over faculty research and place a premium on small class size, some even advertising student-teacher ratios as low as 7:1. For their part, large research institutions also offer seminars in which faculty guide interested students through an intensive examination of a subject.

Seminars usually appear at two points in the curriculum at these large institutions. Some schools provide them in the first year as a way of grabbing students early, making them feel part of the institution and the curriculum, and providing them with a positive educational experience. Freshmen seminars, as they are called, have arisen extensively over the last decade as schools have sought new strategies to increase student retention—that is, the percentage of freshmen who return to the school for a sophomore year and eventually graduate. At the other end, schools may offer seminars for students nearing the end of their undergraduate studies as a way of putting a capstone on their education. These aptly named senior seminars are usually offered by individual departments or majors, and then, most often for students majoring in those subjects. In some cases, senior seminars are reserved for honors students—those students who have done exceptionally well in their major and who are interested in more intensive instruction (and usually a term paper) in exchange for departmental honors on their diploma.

Regardless of where seminars appear in the curriculum or who may enroll, the approach to instruction is often the same. Generally, faculty will assign readings to encourage critical student commentary. In contrast to textbooks that describe a subject, seminar readings are designed to provoke students to consider the "why" questions—why does the author think a certain way, why is it relevant to the subject under consideration, and why should we believe the author (or not)? Then, in class, the instructor will focus on bringing as many students as possible into a discussion of the assigned material. Or, if the focus of the day is on a role-playing exercise, each student will be expected to participate. There are no wallflowers in seminars or small classes, because the classes are intended to be interactive and participatory.

Piecing Together Your Classes

If classes can be taught so differently—in one class you're one of two hundred students listening to a professor lecture all term while in another course you are expected to critique your fifteen classmates' perspectives in discussion—you may begin to wonder if you're really attending classes at the same school. Are the expectations so different in these classes that there is no consistency to your education? It may be tempting to answer yes, but at schools that employ various models of instruction there is actually a progressive pattern to classes. In general, you begin your college education in large, somewhat impersonal classes to gather background material on subjects, and over time, transition to smaller, more intensive classes in which you examine subjects more deeply and interactively. Along the way, you also are likely to get increasing attention from full-time faculty. Sitting in a large introductory history class, you may only be able to make out the vague outlines of your instructor's face at the front of the lecture hall, but by the time you have several history courses under your belt, you'll find yourself in smaller classes interacting directly with that same professor.

Mind you, I'm not saying this is right. If cost were not an issue, you would be best served by taking small, interactive classes with professors who are actively engaged in research and who are interested in translating this work to undergraduates still learning the basic terminology of the subject. Still, I'm not sure that I can think of a single school that provides this kind of instruction across the board, which means that you will need to put together your classes on your own. The key is to seek challenging, interactive, and personal attention from instructors who are engaged in the subjects they are teaching. Fortunately, you can get this in several forms: seek out small seminars, look for interesting discussion sections, and (as I describe later in this chapter) religiously attend your instructor's office hours. A good undergraduate education is not limited to small liberal arts colleges. In fact, one of my best classes in college was a large political philosophy course I had as a freshman. I can barely remember what the professor said in lecture, but the teaching assistant I had for discussion sections was superb. He knew the material, had a way of making hundred-year-old material relevant, and overall was a kind and interesting soul. Today, he is a famous professor, but back when I had him he was just a graduate student dedicated to teaching.

Most large schools have lots of graduate students like these, so don't fret if at first your most personal interactions in the classroom are with teaching assistants. To be blunt, this is why the tuition at large state schools is less expensive than at private liberal arts colleges. Students at the latter may consistently receive a more personalized education, but if you look at the big picture, the experience at a large university may be just as interesting and important. There is something to be said for attending college at a vast, vibrant institution where faculty are engaged in cutting-edge research, students are offered opportunities to participate in these projects, and the extracurricular options are numerous and varied. This is why students may prefer attending schools like Ohio State, the University of Washington, or the University of Kansas. But—and this is a very big but—if you want the same kind of attentive, nurturing, and personalized education that students find at small liberal arts colleges, it will be up to you to patch together these kinds of learning opportunities. You must avoid massive lecture courses wherever possible, research the teaching evaluations of your would-be instructors to find those who care most about undergraduate instruction, and make it your point to attend class, do the reading, and participate in discussions both in and outside of the classroom. In fact, no matter where you attend school, those should be your top priorities. Whether your goal is to learn the most, be bored the least, or get the most out of your tuition dollars (or some combination of the three) there are certain rules to follow to maximize your college experience.

The First Rule—Go to Class

The filmmaker Woody Allen once said that 80 percent of life is just showing up.[1] If this were true, then merely attending class would earn you a B–. Of course, that's not the case (at least in college), but it is still crucial that you attend class on a regular basis. Why do I say this for lecture courses when I've just spent several pages criticizing the teaching of professors who lecture at students rather than engaging them in an interactive process? I've got two answers for you—one idealistic and the other practical (or cynical), depending on your preference. Even in classes in which the professor lectures off PowerPoint slides, there is plenty of material that needs to be taken in, understood, and synthesized for students to say they have learned the subject.

Ideally, the instructor would work harder to help students analyze and apply the information—a process that is best accomplished through interactive exercises. But even if you will be left to your own devices to do this work, attending lectures will help you to understand the material covered. If you're paying close attention, you also may learn how to apply the material by following the examples offered by the professor. Research suggests that we learn through multiple mechanisms,[2] meaning that just listening to your instructor describe concepts similar to the those found in the reading will help you to understand what the various points are and how they are linked together.

If you're fortunate to have a professor who leads an interactive classroom—with discussions of the material, opportunities to apply it, and even role playing exercises—you assuredly will be offered sufficient means to learn the material. But perhaps more importantly, this kind of teaching is what interests and inspires students. Ultimately, you should be looking for content that grabs you, whether as introduction to a possible profession or as an avocational interest to follow in the years ahead. You simply cannot get that kind of intellectual energy, or at least the same level of excitement, by doing the assigned readings on your own and avoiding class.

If none of this convinces you to attend class, then here is the more practical concern: professors routinely offer tidbits in class that will help you on exams. Some of this is the natural process of teaching, as faculty tend to test on the material they cover, both in the readings and in the classroom. Even I have been known to include a test question about an unusual point I know was only covered in class. Call it a reward for those students who regularly come to class. The reality is that many professors do this, and you'll only benefit from the practice if you attend class. For that matter, at some schools students receive points just for attending class and deductions for unexcused absences. If you can boost your class grade simply by sitting in a seat for fifty minutes at a time, why not do so?

Yes, I know the answer to that question. There are lots of potential distractions at college. Road trips, hangovers, boyfriends, girlfriends, and sports all conspire to keep students out of the classroom. Few, if any, of your instructors expect that you will be present for every class in a semester. But you are taking a real risk if you miss more than four sessions in a class that meets twice per week over a fourteen-week semester. That would be the normal meeting schedule for most courses. Needless to say, if you are in a seminar that meets once per week for two or three hours at a time, missing more than two class sessions over a semester is a problem. The more classes you miss, the harder it will be to make up and understand the material and the less likely your professor will be willing to offer you any benefit of the doubt should your final grade sit on the cusp between two marks. Unless your absence is the result of forces beyond your control (for example, illness, a family emergency, or military service), do not expect your instructor to dedicate much time to you at the end of the semester to help answer your questions from the classes you missed earlier in the term.

I've had students tell me that they think they can get all they need from a lecture course by borrowing notes from a classmate. In some classes, instructors even post their own lecture notes or PowerPoint presentations on a shared electronic site (like Blackboard). If the course is a straight lecture class—that is, the instructor simply lectures at students, who write down what is said—there may be some merit to the students' contentions. But even here there are three risks in not attending class. First, you're banking on the prospect that your classmates take notes as well as or better than you. This is not always a good bet, if only because you may not understand their shorthand or thought processes and will miss important material that your friends understood but you cannot recognize from the notes. Second, a professor's posted lecture notes rarely will include answers to questions raised by students in class. Oftentimes, these questions reflect ambiguities or uncertainties that others have about the material, which the professor is able to resolve. If you're not in class, you'll never know what these answers were. Finally, I go back to the multiple ways that we each learn. If you rely solely on the reading and typed lectured notes, you are unlikely to appreciate the way that all of the class concepts fit together. Do yourself a favor and go to class.

Where to Sit

Walking into a classroom, students initially face the question of where to sit. In a small seminar room, this has an easy answer, for the chairs are often scattered around a circular or rectangular table so that everyone faces one another. In a larger class, however—especially in a spacious lecture hall—where should you sit? The short answer is to pick a spot close enough to the front that you can see and hear the teacher while also being able to hear and follow questions and comments offered by other students throughout the classroom. If your professor employs a seating chart, make a point of trying out different spots before choices become permanent. Where do you learn most effectively? Can you ignore distractions while sitting in the back, or do you need to be up front for the instruction to seem more lively? Do you feel you're missing something by sitting in the first few rows since you cannot see how the rest of the class is reacting to the material? The possibilities are as unique as you are. A quick recommendation, though: once you have figured out what works best for you, try to sit near that spot on a regular basis. From a professor's perspective, it is easier to remember students' names, their perspectives, and their willingness to participate in class discussion if we can anticipate where to find them in the classroom.

These recommendations aside, some students instinctively seem to gravitate to two spots in a classroom: the front or the back. Not surprisingly, the front of the class usually finds the most eager students, those who are nodding along with the instructor, taking diligent notes, and asking questions or chiming in with comments when confused or prompted. I know why they're seated in the front—it's easier for them to follow the discussion and engage with me if they're in close proximity— but ideally, I would spread these students out around the classroom.

The other end of the classroom, the last few rows, often finds students who are among the least engaged—surfing the Internet, texting friends, or even talking with others or sleeping. I've never really understood why students come to class only to sleep. I'm not talking about the occasional class in which a student who has been burning the candle at both ends accidentally nods off when a professor begins to drone on. This has happened in my classes a few times, especially to students who have had to work at night to pay for their tuition. That's understandable on an occasional basis. The real problem lies with students who come to class knowing they are not going to take notes or pay attention but for some reason feel compelled to be in class anyway.

To a professor, a sleeping student is horribly disrespectful, and not in the way you might immediately think. Of course, there is the implicit message that we must be really boring to put a student to sleep, but more importantly, a sleeping student says to the rest of the class that they are wasting their time in paying attention. So if you come to class—and, really, you must to do well—come prepared to pay attention. If you find yourself regularly surfing the Internet, talking to others, or even sleeping, you need to do some serious soul searching to figure out why this is happening. Perhaps the class is a requirement with no alternatives, in which case you'll have to suck it up. But if the course really is that boring, see if you can switch to a different section. Or, if you have the gumption, talk with the instructor before or after class to register your concerns. A good professor will appreciate this feedback to help make the material more approachable for you. If you find yourself distracted in many of your classes, then perhaps you're pursuing the wrong subjects or the school is a bad fit for you. In some cases, college may not even be right for you. If you're going to spend the time and money to attend college, you ought to do your best to get the most out of it.

The Second Rule—Do the Reading

On the first day of the semester, the professor will hand out a syllabus for the class. In some cases, the syllabus may be available online or even e-mailed to you in the weeks before the semester begins. A syllabus is a kind of guidebook for the class, providing an overview of what the course will cover, explaining the course requirements and grading formula, outlining the various days' activities, and detailing the reading assignments that are associated with each class session. The syllabus will identify the books you need to purchase and provide information on where you can obtain articles or other materials assigned as reading.

Students often ask me when they should begin the reading for their course. I usually get these questions in early May, when returning students have signed up for their fall classes and want to know what the reading list will be so they can get started on the reading over the summer. I may face the revocation of my PhD for saying this, but I actually do not recommend that students do advance reading over the summer. Summer should be a time to relax and recharge, to explore new and different interests, not a time to worry about getting ahead. Plus, it's likely that you will forget the fine details of what you read in June for a class that will cover the material in October. There is certainly nothing wrong with reading the material ahead of time, but if you're really committed to staying on top of your coursework, you'll have to go back to those reading assignments during the semester to remind yourself of what they covered.

It would be a professor's ideal world if his greatest worry were students who wanted to complete the reading months ahead of time. Regretfully, the reality is almost always the opposite. It's as if faculty have become oral surgeons, pulling teeth to encourage students to complete the assigned reading. In nearly two decades in the classroom, I've sensed that the problem has been getting worse, and I'm not sure why. I suspect that we're seeing more students who come to college for professional reasons, not for their interest in learning; as a result, they may not appreciate the connection between the reading and their professional goals. Also, as students spend progressively more time in front of a screen—be it television, video games, or the Internet—books and articles may appear "boring" to more of them. Faculty are continually looking for new strategies to interest and engage students, and we're constantly trying to keep pace with developing technologies that more vividly illustrate the course themes. That said, a central part of any class involves reading. No matter the class, it is a virtual certainty that you cannot excel at, let alone pass the course, if you ignore the reading or don't do it carefully.

Different Kinds of Reading Assignments

Readings often can be divided into two categories—those that tell or explain and those that offer ideas or findings to spur further thought. Textbooks almost always fall into the first category and are most likely to be assigned in introductory classes. In these classes, instructors are trying to convey baseline knowledge to you—the distinguishing characteristics of geological forms, the various components of macroeconomic demand, the parts of the brain that influence mood. Readings, then, introduce you to concepts and facts and explain what they mean, why they are important, and how they fit together. To ignore these readings is to miss the very building blocks of the class and discipline that will follow.

I know some students believe they can get by without completing the reading so long as they show up to each class and take detailed notes from the professor. In truth, they can in some courses. Unfortunately, some instructors simply lecture from the textbook, essentially describing or reiterating the various points made in the reading. What's the point of getting the same material twice, students may ask? It's hard to argue with this complaint; instructors are doing a real disservice to their students if they choose simply to spoon feed the readings to the class. I suspect some teachers are concerned about the poor reading habits of their students and, in order to ensure that everyone begins with a basic grounding in the subject matter, choose to describe the readings again in class. But this penalizes the conscientious students while rewarding the slackers. Moreover, research shows that you will learn more through hands-on application of concepts than rote lecturing.

Still, even if your professor tends to "lecture from the book," it's a good idea to complete the reading and come to class. You're likely to miss some facts and concepts by relying on one delivery method, so think of the combination as a backstop to your education, allowing you to spot which parts of the material you're uncertain about so you can seek clarification. You'll also be in a better position to pose your own informed questions that challenge the professor and show him just how much you are learning in the class.

Fortunately, most professors use the readings as a jumping-off point for further discussion in class—even in introductory classes that focus on basic concepts. Imagine yourself in an introductory class on political theory (my very first class in college). Sure, you could rely on the readings to understand why Thomas Hobbes believed that life is "nasty, brutish, and short," and you could even go to class to hear your professor put Hobbes in context with other philosophers of his time. But I doubt you could apply Hobbes's theory to your life problems or distinguish his approach from that of others unless you had guided practice in the implications and differences of these theories. For that matter, you would hardly be in a position to practice analyzing and applying those theories unless you first had read about them before coming to class. I promise you that the best, most interesting classes are those in which you're encouraged to "play" with the concepts in class, even in introductory courses. But those courses all presuppose that you have completed the readings before coming to class; otherwise, you risk simply being lost.

If introductory courses rely heavily on descriptive readings in textbooks, the readings in other classes are designed to introduce you to debates in the field and encourage you to develop your own "take" on the questions. In a class on criminology, an instructor might assign you dueling articles on the causes of crime—whether crime is the result of environmental influences or the personal failings of criminals. Don't worry—your professor isn't expecting you to digest a half-century's worth of writings and come to class with a definite view on the subject. Rather, she is hoping to provide you with a window on the big debates in the field and push you to analyze the arguments by identifying the strengths and weaknesses in the articles. To ignore these readings is to confine yourself to a blind struggle in the classroom. You may eventually pick up the main points of the readings by listening to your instructor and classmates discuss the selections, but you cannot be sure that you've truly understood them. Nor will you be able to participate in the discussion, as you won't know ahead of time what people are talking about.

Required versus Optional Reading

As I said, the second rule of class is to complete the readings. How you do this is a matter of practice. On many syllabi professors will distinguish between required and recommended or optional assignments. Needless to say, you ought to complete the required readings; ideally, do so a few days before the class in which they will be covered so that your memory about them is fresh. With respect to the optional readings, let me make another confession: I never completed these readings as an undergraduate. Frankly, I found it a challenge just to keep up with the required assignments while also trying to maintain a life outside of class. Did I miss out on a fuller education by failing to tackle the optional readings? Probably. Has it been fatal? Not that I can tell. Frankly, I've never quite understood why professors list the optional readings, at least on syllabi for undergraduate courses. If you're really interested in a subject and have the time, of course you should take up the optional readings. But if the teacher is a good one, he will not hold you responsible for knowing their content, and it shouldn't hurt your course grade if you are unable to read them.

How to Keep Up with the Reading

I say that I felt challenged as an undergraduate to keep up with the required readings. This doesn't necessarily mean you will be, for I was—and still am—a relatively slow reader. But at the start of each semester you ought to set aside more time than you anticipate necessary to complete your readings before class. As a general rule, faculty figure on one to two hours of student preparation for each hour spent in class. So if you're taking a three-credit class, start by blocking out at least six, and ideally nine, hours per week to complete the course readings. In all likelihood, you won't need all of this time. But until you have a handle on how difficult the reading is for a particular class and how long it will typically take to work your way through it, give yourself the luxury of not worrying about the time. In my own case, I came to recognize that I read at a rate of sixty pages an hour if the articles or books weren't technical, but my rate dropped by half if the material was from a textbook or involved complicated formulas or ideas. By determining your own rate, you'll be able to set aside enough time each week to get your reading done.

Reading for Content

If you have made it to college, I presume that you learned strategies in high school to read actively for content. That is, you need to think of reading for class as an interactive process in which you first look over the entire assignment, then read through it, and finally combine a technique of underlining and/or note taking to prompt yourself about the main points of the piece. You'll want to highlight key terms, important names and dates, and the definitions of central concepts and theories. Then, you may want to jot down notes to yourself that explain how certain concepts relate to one another or raise interesting questions.

In my day as an undergrad, we regularly highlighted our textbooks with colored pens and scribbled notes to ourselves in the margin. Today, however, students may read their books online or be reluctant to mark up textbooks in order to sell them back at the end of the semester. Regardless of which approach you employ, it is important to take active notes as you read, whether electronically, on a separate sheet of paper, or in the book itself. To provide a concrete example, I've pasted below a section from a book I published several years ago on hate speech regulation. The selection comes from a chapter that discusses the courts' treatment of hate speech. Now, imagine that you are taking a class from me on the First Amendment and we're going to discuss whether hate speech warrants protection under the First Amendment as free speech. Here is how I would tackle the reading for that topic if I were a student preparing for that class. You'll note that in addition to highlighting some of the text, I also have written some notes in the margin:

Free speech and open discourse are privileged rights under the First Amendment. According to the courts, the First Amendment applies to "expression," a term that is generally considered to mean speech. Certainly, some actions can be expressive, including the burning of the flag (*Texas v. Johnson*), a draft card (*Bond v. Floyd*), or the donning of offensive apparel (*Cohen v. California*), but for the most part the courts have distinguished between speech, which is expressive and thus constitutionally protected, and actions, which are neither.

> *1st A = expression*
> *Speech & some acts*
>
> *Know the cases?*
> *Texas v. Johnson*
> *Bond v. Floyd*
> *Cohen v. Calif*

Historically, there have been only five bases under which the courts are willing to restrict speech: obscenity; libel; time, place and manner regulations; the clear and present danger test; and fighting words. Obscenity law probably traces back to our Puritan past, reflecting the notion that some expression is so carnal and salacious that it may be regulated. Libel is a branch of defamation law, allowing individuals to sue those who knowingly malign their reputations. Time, place and manner restrictions are just as they sound, permitting public bodies to place reasonable limits on the way in which expression is delivered, rather than its content. A protestor may not blare his message outside your bedroom window at two in the morning, although he is free to express his views at a more reasonable time and place. Similarly, under the clear and present danger test, courts have been willing to punish expression that imminently incites others to criminal or dangerous activity (*Brandenburg v. Ohio*). The classic example is yelling "fire" in a crowded theater, where the speaker's interest in expression is overwhelmed by the threat of people being trampled on the way out. Courts interpret this test very narrowly, with only the most egregious speech qualifying as dangerous. Finally, fighting words statutes are said to protect the public peace. First recognized by the Supreme Court in the 1942 case of *Chaplinsky v. New Hampshire*, the term was initially defined as words that "by their very utterance inflict injury" and "tend to incite an immediate breach of the peace." However, over time this definition has been winnowed so that by the mid-1960s it included only the latter half-speech that incites an immediate breach of the peace.

> *5 bases to restrict*
>
> *1. Obscenity*
>
> *2. Libel*
> *What's defam?*
>
> *3. TPM*
>
> *4. C&P Danger*
> *Brandenburg v. OH*
> *Narrow interp.*
>
> *5. Fighting Words*
> *Chaplinsky v. NH*
> *2nd half of test now*

I would begin by looking over the entire selection to see that it introduces the bases for legal restrictions on speech. This helps in comprehending the selection, because you then have an idea of what to expect before you read each of the lines. Next, I would highlight or underline terms or definitions and the text that explains them. So in the first paragraph, I've highlighted the part that discusses the basis of First Amendment protection (speech and some expressive acts). In the second paragraph, I have marked the five areas of speech that may be regulated and their definitions. I also have highlighted all cases that are named, since, as a student, I might be required to understand their holdings in a class discussion of constitutional law.

I suspect you are familiar with this form of highlighting, and some of you may have a variety of highlighters at hand to mark up your reading. In fact, I knew one student who used different colors for highlighting her readings—one color for background information, another for definitions, and a third color for the ramifications or consequences of the main points. I do not necessarily recommend this approach—it is a bit compulsive, after all—but the instinct is a good one, ensuring that you can distinguish between the main ideas of a reading selection and the implications of those points.

If you look in the right margin, you'll see that I also have written notes to myself that help to summarize and organize the selection. In the second paragraph, for example, I have broken out the five bases for speech restrictions into a list as a way to help me remember what each of the possible items is. Where a definition would not have been immediately clear to me as a first-time reader or where the basis for the restriction has changed over time, I've put a note in the margin to prompt me to ask about the issue in class or to recall that legal restrictions are often evolving.

So for example, I wrote "narrow interp." next to the clear and present danger test to remind me that that the courts have found only a limited class of "dangerous" speech worthy of restriction. Similarly, I wrote "2nd half of test now" next to fighting words to help me recall that the test initially issued in *Chaplinsky v. New Hampshire* for fighting words has since been cut in half by subsequent decisions. I've also abbreviated a longer legal test—time, place, and manner restrictions—into "TPM" in the margin, because I've learned that I'm more likely to remember a term if I can create an acronym. Finally, I have added two questions in the margin. In the first paragraph where the selection lists a group of cases, I've noted that students might be expected to know these cases. Undoubtedly, the discussion in class would help me to figure this out. But if the answer were not obvious, then I would need to ask the professor whether he expected us to know these cases by name and holding or whether they were provided in the reading merely for illustrative purposes. In addition, I've highlighted a point that might not have been clear to me from the passage. Libel may be a subset of defamation law, but the reading does not (in this small selection) explain what defamatory expression may be. Here, I would need to ask the professor in class to get this question answered.

Anticipate the Questions

Completing the reading, while a necessary prerequisite, is not sufficient on its own for you to be prepared for class. The final step is to anticipate how the reading will be applied in class. In the selection above, it should be obvious that the professor wants students to understand which kinds of speech can be restricted and on what bases. But knowing the legal tests does not necessarily mean that students will understand how to apply the definitions to particular fact patterns. So before coming to class, I might start to envision factual scenarios that would implicate these tests. Suppose someone was calling me nasty names from the street outside my office at noon. Could the police arrest or cite the speaker for disturbing the peace? What if he were using cymbals on my front yard at 7:00 a.m.? If the professor is worth her salt, she will hardly leave these legal bases to the mere words of their definitions. Instead, she'll want students to try applying the definitions in order to appreciate the theories behind, and limits of, the speech restrictions.

In other courses, it may not be as obvious how the reading will be applied in class. If, for example, you're reading a biology textbook on cell division, it's likely that the next class session will be dedicated to the process of cellular replication, but you may not be able to predict what issues will come up in lecture or discussion. A good way of preparing for these classes is to review the questions posed in the margins or at the ends of relevant sections in your textbook. Virtually every textbook has these questions, which are designed to help you synthesize the material just read. Regardless of whether these precise issues will be raised in class, going over them ahead of time will ensure that you are prepared to get the most out of the lecture or discussion planned.

Preparing like this does not mean that you need to come to class with a clear understanding of the reading or a practiced ability to apply the lessons of the assigned text. There is plenty of room for confusion in reading class assignments, and in fact, a good professor will reassure students that they do not have to "get" either the reading or class discussion at first. Rather, the challenge of a good course and, indeed, the responsibilities of a good professor and dedicated students, are to be willing to wade through the confusion in order to build understanding. So if you make it through the reading and cannot seem to understand what it means or how it might be applied, don't worry at first.

Instead, come to class prepared to explain what you do not understand and why you are confused. This way your professor can help you to make sense of the reading. If you show up saying, "I read the assignment but it's confusing," your teacher will have little insight into your confusion. By contrast, if you were to say, "I read about speech restrictions, and I don't get the difference between fighting words and libel," he would be in a much better position to help allay your concerns and lead you to a broader understanding of the reading. In addition, your question would show him that you really had tackled the reading, motivating the professor even more to help you resolve the question. Many professors have little tolerance for students who fail to complete the reading and then expect them to explain what it means. The classroom is a two-way street. My colleagues and I are there to help you, but only if you complete your end of the bargain and come to class prepared and willing to learn.

The Third Rule—Take Notes

When I look out at a full classroom, I expect to see students poised either with pen in hand or fingers on keyboard. I'm hardly under the impression that students should be copying down my every word, but if they expect to recall the material covered in class, they need to take effective notes. Unless you have a verified disability, most professors will not permit you to record the class, so you're going to have to rely on your own note taking to create a record of classroom instruction. Years ago, we might have permitted tape recordings of class, especially for students who expected to miss a class session because of an unavoid-able conflict. But in this era of web content, the cautious professor does not permit recording, lest his lectures be posted online where others may employ his intellectual property without compensation. (Don't laugh. It has happened.)

I presume that you have had practice taking notes in high school, but the amount you'll be expected to record and recall in college is greater. Some professors provide students a summary of important points they'll cover in each day's class, and I know of others who even post their lec-ture notes on a class intranet. More likely, however, you'll come to class not knowing what the professor is going to cover that day and will need to take notes as discussion unfolds.

Note Taking in Lectures

In a lecture class, you may be tempted to write down almost every-thing the professor says, but this misses the purpose of note taking. Instead, you should be listening for key points and terms, which you should copy down along with any definitions that follow. Then, pay attention to how the professor discusses those concepts. Is her point about the limitations of the terms? Does she describe how the theories developed or why people support them? Does she link terms or con-cepts together? Whatever her point, your goal is to figure out *why* the terms are mentioned, *what* they mean, *where* they are applicable, and *how* they are important. But more than understanding the answers to those questions, you need to be able to explain them well enough so that the future you who looks at these notes in the weeks ahead will appreciate the points.

Note Taking in Seminars or Discussion Sections

Note taking during student discussions or seminars is different, for presumably you don't need to copy down everything that your class-mates have to say. Here, the goal of the course is to encourage you to apply the concepts presented. So put your pen down or close your lap-top, and see if you can appreciate the arguments raised and the extent and limitations of the ideas being discussed. If an argument strikes you as solid, make a note of it and your reaction. If others seem weak, write down why you think them insufficient. Pay close attention to points that connect to others raised previously in the class or those that involve the readings, as these signal the kind of overarching themes that your instructor is seeking to build. If you are fortunate to have an instructor who closes each class session by summarizing the day's discussion, you should include that summary in your notes as a synopsis of what the teacher considers to be most relevant. By no means must you agree with your classmates (or even your professor) on the substance of these points—indeed, the point of discussion sections or seminars is to encourage independent thought. But when it comes to exam time, you need to recognize which themes or issues your professor considers central to the course (more on exams in the next chapter).

Synthesizing Your Notes

Note taking does not end when you walk out the classroom door. You also need to set aside some time after class to read over and synthesize your notes while they are fresh in your mind. If you don't, you face that dreaded prospect of sitting down at the end of the semester to study for exams, only to read through your classroom scribbles with little idea about what you wrote or why the notes are relevant. Your post-class synthesis should take no more than fifteen minutes, and it's time definitely well spent. Focus on three things. First, make sure you have written down a ready definition for all terms, concepts, theories, or processes covered in class (or described in the reading assigned for that day's session). Second, check to see that you understand why these elements are relevant and that your notes provide explanations that you'll be able to follow in the weeks ahead. Finally, make sure your notes reflect how these terms and ideas are linked.

Let me give you an example. Suppose you're enrolled in a class on water science and the day's topic concerns the effects of agricultural runoff on water quality. Examining your notes at the end of the day, you would want to make sure you understood what chemicals or elements are found in agricultural runoff (for example, nitrogen, fertilizers, and manure), how they can leach into ambient water, and what effects they have—and why—when they reach the local water supply. All of these subjects presumably would have been covered in class, which, if you were paying attention, you likely included in your notes. By taking a few extra minutes at the end of a class session to synthesize your notes, you can capture these points effectively and clearly so that you'll be able to study more easily when it comes time for an exam. If for some reason your notes are missing any of these parts, you will still have time to go back to your instructor, the reading, or even one of your classmates to clarify the points while they are fresh in your mind. Taking a few minutes at the end of each class will save you lots of time and limit your anxiety and frustration later in the semester.

One final point about note taking: if you are ever absent from a class, make sure to borrow notes from a classmate. Your professors are not responsible for providing you with copies of their lecture notes, and they may not even use notes in a seminar or discussion section. For everyone's sake, don't sidle up to your professor before class and ask that infamous question, "Did I miss anything important while I was away?" Although most instructors are too well mannered to say so, I can promise you they are secretly toying with one of two snarky answers. If you ever hear, "Yes, I went over the secrets to the final exam," or "No, I'm just here to listen to my own voice," you'll know that you've encountered a professor who has heard this silly question too many times. Most students who ask it don't intend to offend, but the question showcases a misunderstanding of students' responsibilities for their own education. If you're ill for an extended amount or time or must miss class because of a family emergency, most professors will work with you to catch up in the course. But if you simply decided to skip class, the responsibility is yours to pick up on what you missed.

The Fourth Rule—Remain an Active Participant in Class

Depending on the class you take, participation may be a part of your grade. At a liberal arts college where I've taught, class participation figured prominently in final grades—upwards of 25 percent. By contrast, at a large research university where I taught more recently, academic administrators declared that faculty could not factor class participation into course grades, but we could take account of attendance. I'm still not sure of the logic of that rule.

Just showing up for class is a poor substitute for class participation. Not just because the measure of a student's performance in a course should account for her involvement in the enterprise, but also because you will learn more and your classes will be much more interesting if you make a point of joining the discussion. I recognize that this is easier said than done. In large lecture courses the instruction is sometimes set up to discourage student questions, and, of course, some students are naturally shyer than others.

Several years ago I was a college freshman, sitting in an introductory economics course taught in a lecture hall of more than two hundred students by a lone figure on a stage who was barely visible without the aid of binoculars. If the professor had stopped to entertain every student question, he never would have gotten through his lecture notes. But even this professor had a policy of encouraging students to submit questions throughout the lecture by passing notes to the stage. I presume his theory was that the anonymity of written questions would permit even the shyest students to ask questions if they were confused. Unfortunately for him, the technique backfired, giving the class clowns license to send the oddest questions to the stage, which, to the professor's credit, he actually answered. We heard explanations for why he wore the loud, clashing ties he had purchased decades earlier, why he owned a Russian fur hat that traveled with him everywhere, and even what he thought of the argument that Keynesian economics was just Marxism dressed up for polite society. Although the questions threw the professor off his lecture, at the same time they humanized a man who otherwise seemed pretty dry.

Ask Questions

As you undoubtedly have surmised, I despise large classes in which professors simply lecture at students, and I regularly challenge my colleagues to make even the largest classes interactive. That, of course, is the theory behind the small discussion sections that often accompany lecture classes, but even in those large lecture halls you need to be willing to stop faculty to ask questions if you're confused. It is patently unfair and a waste of your money for a school essentially to say, "Sit still and listen to the great professor pontificate but wait until the discussion section for a graduate student to answer your questions." If you're confused, if you wonder how a concept being presented relates to other classwork or even the world around you, make the professor stop and respond to your question. The best instructors will adore you for it. It tells them that someone in the audience is paying attention, that the class is composed of real students instead of passive consumers, and it reminds instructors of the ultimate goal of classes—sparking an intellectual dialogue with their students. From the students' perspective, not only will you get your questions answered, but the break provided by your query may divert the instructor from a canned lecture so that the dynamic in the classroom changes from one-way communication to a conversation.

Outside of large lectures, there is really no excuse for not participating in class discussion. This is where the real learning takes place as you work with your instructor to tease out the ramifications and limits of the topics covered. Simply sitting in your seat and remaining mute while others around you talk is the difference between watching a neighborhood softball game and actually taking the field. The former might give you some ideas about the rules of the game, but you won't learn the skills necessary to play it by sitting on the sidelines.

Why Participate?

I can hear some of you now objecting, wondering what's to be gained in discussing, say, the laws of physics when the smart student should simply copy down the formulas that explain how velocity is measured. The answer is threefold, moving from the ideal to the practical. First, even the most "technical" subjects—the ones that seem to be based on formulas, laws, or equations—are very much open for debate. Researchers continually seek to understand *why* the world operates as it does, *what* the implications are of these formulas, and *how* far the analogies extend. By taking a particular class, you are joining the line of scholars who have studied the topic. Sure, you need to get down the basic terminology, but after that the real practice of learning is trying to understand a discipline's breadth. That is where questioning comes in. By asking questions, by participating in the class discussion, you're satisfying the most basic reason for coming to college and taking those classes—your own intellectual curiosity.

The second, more practical reason for participating in class discussion is to ensure that you actually understand the material covered. Time and again research has shown that people learn the most when instruction is participatory. Having me explain to you, for example, the basis for a constitutional doctrine may cause you to scribble down an explanation in your notes, but could you readily apply that doctrine to a new set of facts if you hadn't practiced it in class? What if I'm unclear in my explanation? What if the examples I'm using at first don't make sense to you? What if you're curious about the possible exceptions to the doctrine described? If you don't pipe up and ask your questions, if you don't practice applying the concepts presented, you're simply not going to have as strong a command of the class material as you should.

And that leads us to the most utilitarian reason for participating in class—your final grade. I can assure you that the students who do best in a class are those who participate most actively. Not only are they the ones who understand the course material best—because they have had their questions answered—but they also get the benefit of the doubt when a teacher has to decide between a B+ or an A−. They pick up all the points on the syllabus for class participation, and their names and faces stick with the instructor as the students who tried the hardest. Even in a class of more than two hundred students taught five years ago, I can still tell you the names of the top ten students I could regularly count on to ask good questions and challenge me to explain the material more clearly. And I know many teachers who can say the same thing.

How to Participate

There is an art to classroom participation, one you may have picked up from your days in high school. Essentially, when you walk into a classroom each day, you're issued a limited number of chances to raise your hand and ask or answer a question. The larger the course, the fewer chances you get. In a course of more than one hundred students, you may have just one or two opportunities per week, if that. In a seminar of seven students, you'll be expected to participate upwards of ten times in an hour. So, just as Oliver Cromwell was reported to have said, keep your powder dry and use your opportunities to speak when you are truly confused about a concept or when the idea in your head will truly advance class discussion. Professors can name the few students in any class who seem to have their hands up throughout the entire session. You don't want to be one of those folks. Some students talk just to hear their voices, whereas others seem never to have learned the benefits of sharing when in kindergarten. You should participate just enough for your instructor to know and recognize you while leaving sufficient opportunities for your classmates to chime in.

What should you do if you are shy? Certainly, some students are shyer than others; I've even come across students who sweat and turn red at the prospect of talking in a class of twenty students. Some of the responsibility here is yours: you need to push yourself a bit to participate in the class. But push does not mean shove. A good instructor will recognize students who appear unsure and will put the clearest, most obvious questions to them just so the students can practice lending their voice in class. Or, if you're worried about the joining the discussion, listen for the questions posed by the professor and challenge yourself to at least raise your hand when you think you know the answer. If this is still too much, stop the professor after class or see him during office hours and introduce yourself. Ask the professor a question about the day's class session. Make this a habit so that the teacher begins to understand who you are and can help to clear up any lingering questions you might have from the day's session. Pretty soon it won't seem as daunting to continue that conversation during the class.

The Fifth Rule—Go to Office Hours

On almost every syllabus, a professor will list his or her office hours. Coming from high school, where you may never have visited with a teacher after class, this may seem like a foreign concept. At college, instructors are usually required to reserve one to four hours per week to be available to meet with students. Most of these meetings are in the professor's office—hence the term "office hours"—but I also know instructors who host these sessions at local coffee houses or restaurants. Sadly, way too few students ever take advantage of these opportunities. In fact, for many of my colleagues, office hours are penciled into their schedules as assumed "down time" because students rarely come to meet. Why is this so? Many students undoubtedly believe that their education stops at the classroom walls. "I do the reading, go to class, write my papers and take my exams," they think. "I didn't sign up for more work." Others likely think that office hours are for the students having trouble in a class. "If I'm not falling behind, why do I need to go visit with the professor for remedial instruction?" they may think. Still more students may be intimidated by their instructors, imagining that a professor will look down upon them for not knowing as much about the subject as the teacher.

Getting Your Money's Worth

All of the reasons listed above are flat-out wrong—or at least they ought to be. As I continually tell students, office hours are where you really get your money's worth at college, especially in large classes. Think for a moment about the ratio between professor and students in a three hundred–person class. How much of the professor's time and attention are you getting? Not much. How reasonable is it to think that the professor knows how you learn, what you understand, and what's still confusing about the class? Pretty unreasonable. But if you stop by during office hours you can have the professor's undivided attention. Not understanding a concept? Here is your chance for one-on-one instruction. Curious about how the course material relates to another area? You can explore the possibilities with your professor. Notice that the professor plays drums in a local jazz band and want to shoot the breeze about an up-and-coming artist? You'll have an eager audience.

It may be hard to appreciate, but most professors—even famous senior faculty—like mentoring students. We welcome the chance to talk with you, especially about subjects of mutual interest. That's one of the reasons that we chose this line of work. Many students at small liberal arts colleges seem instinctively to get this point. There, the metaphorical distance between students and faculty is narrow. By virtue of small classes, students get more faculty attention in class; they see professors around campus and in the community; at some schools, professors even live in the residence halls. It's only natural, then, for students to continue during office hours the conversations they're used to having with professors elsewhere. At these campuses, faculty are available virtually throughout the day.

Yet often at large state schools, students mysteriously seem to peel away from faculty outside of class. Since they're not used to talking with instructors inside the classroom, students seem almost embarrassed to seek out professors during office hours, like it's an awkward blind date and they won't know what to say. Really, don't worry: show up, knock on the door, introduce yourself, and ask a question. We'll take it from there.

Letters of Recommendation

Still not convinced that it's worth your time to attend office hours? Let me resort to another practical consideration—letters of recommendation. In my case, I tell students that I will not write letters of reference unless I know them well. That means they must have taken at least one of my classes, worked hard, and performed to the best of their ability. But it also means that they've given me an insight into their interests.

Perhaps a student was a regular participant in class and willingly shared his thoughts and reactions. Maybe he stayed after class to clarify a point from the discussion. Or more likely, he may have attended office hours, where we talked about his reasons for attending college and his interests postgraduation. Not every professor follows my rule, but having sat on both hiring and admissions committees throughout the years, I can tell you which letters of recommendation will help get you the job. They're the longer, more substantive letters that show the professor knows enough about the student to recommend him. Consider a letter that simply says:

> I had John Smith in my expository writing class two years ago. He earned a B+ in the class, which signifies that he was in the upper third of his classmates. He is undoubtedly a solid student.

Does the writer sound like he knows the student? I don't think so. Would you be convinced to hire the student? Probably not. Now, compare that kind of limited reference to one that says:

> I first had Jane Green in my public policy class three years ago. Since then, she has taken two other courses from me, one a senior seminar. I also have gotten to know Jane through her regular visits to office hours and as an advisor for her independent study. Over that time Jane has refined her focus from a broad interest in public policy to her current involvement in immigration reform.

Whether or not the reference is strong—and it likely will be if the professor took the time to write—the letter establishes the basis for the professor's recommendation. In my own case, I'm convinced that the strongest letter of reference I ever gave was for an A student who got into law school. That may not sound like much of an accomplishment until you consider that the student was in her early thirties, having spent her twenties addicted to crack cocaine and turning tricks as a prostitute to feed her habit. (Yes, this is a true story.) How did I know this about her? It wasn't by reading her mind as she sat in the second row of class. No one at the university sent me a file about her. Rather, she was a regular visitor to office hours. Over the course of a fourteen-week semester, we must have spent ten hours chatting outside of class. She had lots and lots of questions to ask, some about the material we covered in class and others about the implications of the reading. But it wasn't until months into the semester that I began to learn of her past. Over time, we established a professional, respectful relationship in which she felt comfortable talking about the many challenges she had faced before college. And by her opening up, we had several fascinating conversations about the differences between the legal precepts we had discussed as theory in class and their application to her own experiences in the criminal justice system.

I'm certainly not saying that you should invent a dramatic past, nor do you need an interesting back story to get the attention of your professors. Rather, it's the kind of give-and-take that you can enjoy with your professors—with people whose job it is to teach, whether in the classroom or elsewhere on campus—that will help you to grow and will allow your professors to best help you. Our office doors are open. Make the most of your education and stop by.

How to Contact Your Professors

In these days of online communications, many students find it easier to stay in touch with their professors by e-mail. Not only are students used to virtual lives almost from the moment they first learn to type, but it also can be less stressful to deal with an instructor by e-mail than by speaking in person. Certainly, e-mail is a valuable way of communicating with professors when the questions are less complicated and the issues open to quick resolution. If you cannot remember when the term paper is due or you realize you missed a point in your class notes, don't hesitate to send your professor a quick e-mail to ask for clarification. But if the question is more complex—you don't understand a key concept presented over a couple of class sessions or you are considering a withdrawal from the class—you really need to set aside your computer to make an appointment to talk in person.

Supplemental instruction or guidance doesn't lend itself well to a quick response. Would you see a psychologist who only treated you over Twitter? Well, neither should you accept the possibility of thoughtful help or advice by e-mail. Among other things, professors are busy with lots of e-mail each day, and it simply isn't a good use of their time to try to accomplish over the Internet what can be offered more efficiently and effectively in person. Remember that personal attention I keep alluding to—the one-on-one treatment you should be seeking, if not demanding, as a student? You're more likely to get your money's worth if you bring your complicated questions directly to your professors in person.

I'm a little reluctant to use the word "demand" when encouraging you to seek personal attention from your instructors, for I worry about the few students who have not learned the concept of limits. They're the ones accosting faculty after every class with question upon question, following them down to the hall to their offices where they do not leave even when the professor needs to get to his next class. They e-mail around the clock and expect their instructors to respond almost instantaneously. In some cases, they call professors at home to ask questions or even demand to know why the teacher has not answered their e-mails. Believe me, I have seen these students; they're real. So when I say "demand," let's recognize that the concept is one of respectful persistence. Remember that your fellow classmates would like some of the professor's time. Give your instructor a grace period of a day to respond to your e-mail (and even longer if you know she is ill or out of town); limit your visits to office hours unless you've scheduled a different time with the professor; and never, ever contact a professor at home unless she has specifically sanctioned this on the syllabus or in class.

I also need to give you advance warning about the style in which you contact your professors. My guess is that, raised on a regular diet of texting, you're used to a casual approach of communicating by e-mail or cell phone. Trying to advise your friend that you are delayed for lunch, you might text, "Im L8—C U @ 1." This style is perfectly acceptable between friends, and there are some professors who do not mind abbreviated, casual electronic conversations. But you need to remember that for many professors, the ability to write well is an essential skill of a college education. If a professor's first interaction with you is an informal, colloquial e-mail—the kind of message that sounds to an instructor like, "Hey, dude, what's up?"—you risk burning through your intellectual credibility before the professor has truly gotten to know you. The better approach is to treat e-mail correspondence with faculty as you would with a prospective employer: show respect for your professors by writing to them in complete sentences and with proper wording. This does not mean that you need to hire an editor to write your professor an e-mail, but bear in mind that you only get one chance to make a good impression. So when drafting that e-mail, leave out the cutesy abbreviations, and remember to run spell check before hitting send.

EXAMS

I had a good friend in college named Eric. As freshmen we lived on the same dorm floor. We took many of the same classes, often ate at the same table, and once even double-dated. (Unfortunately, we each had our eye on the same woman.) Eric is one of the smartest people I have known—and also one of the most absentminded I have encountered. He was legendary for his inability to manage time, but never more so than the night before our first final exam in college. Many of us were stooped over our books in the dorm's multipurpose room studying for the next day's test, but not Eric. He already knew the material and had decided to go out to a party to relax before the big day. The next morning, we all filed out of the dorm on our way to the exam room, but we didn't see Eric. Where had he gone? No one knew. Then, with one hour left on a three-hour exam, Eric bolted into the room, eyes wild and hair and clothes unkempt. He had slept through his alarm, awakening to the sickening realization that he had already missed more than half of his Economics 101 final.

You're probably expecting a moral from this story in which Eric failed the exam, potentially even the class, and eventually learned his lesson. That would make sense, but as I said, Eric is one of the smartest people I've known. He wrote furiously for the remaining hour of the exam, apparently pushing out some of the snappiest prose then known about macroeconomics, and saved himself and his grade. To our everlasting shock, he earned an A– in the class. Today, he is a comptroller for a major electronics company in California. Every time I see him we relive the story of the final exam that almost wasn't, and even Eric will acknowledge that no one—not even him—should ever follow his example. "I have no idea how I pulled that off," he'll say, "and I never want to find out again."

Eric lived through his very own exam dream while awake; many others are familiar with the nightmare of sitting for a final exam when you haven't taken the course. The terror only gets worse if you find yourself naked in the dream, too. Trust me, if you haven't yet had an exam dream, it's one of the few unpleasant holdovers from college, and I'm sorry to say that it often follows you later into life. But if there is any good news, it's that exam dreams are usually a sign of dedicated students. If you weren't afraid of showing up for a final exam unprepared, then it wouldn't be in your subconscious.

Of course, my goal here is to minimize the chances that your nighttime terror becomes a daytime reality, and in fact, that task is not as hard as it may seem at first. If you have been attending class, if you have been doing the reading and taking notes, then the chances that you will fail are miniscule. As I think back over the students who ever have earned a D or F from me in a class, all I can remember are the students who blew off the reading, did not come to class, were daydreaming on the rare occasions they were present, or who failed to come talk to me when they were likely confused about the material. It may sound like a tautology, but just going through the motions of being a student is likely to build enough understanding of the course material to see you through to a passing grade in a class.

A Word (or Two) about Grades

If you're reading this book, however, a satisfactory grade is not likely what you're hoping to achieve. The days of the "gentleman's C"—the notion that a C was a respectable grade that still prepared students for professional success—are long gone. You likely want an A in your classes or, at the very worst, a B. If so, you're hardly alone. Students today are increasingly dissatisfied with any grade lower than a B–, and some are quite vocal in their wishes. I know of colleagues who spend the weeks following each semester stuck in their offices explaining to students why they deserved the grade they received and, if necessary, recalculating scores to ensure that the grades were entered accurately. But grade inflation, as we call it, is hardly the fault of students alone. It also owes to the nasty creep-creep-creep of college administrators, who, defensive over rising tuition costs, now fret about appeasing students and their parents. I even have heard some colleges administrators speak of students, not mockingly, as customers.

Grade Inflation

One need only look at GPAs at a variety of schools to recognize that grades have been on the rise for more than a decade now. At an Ivy League school like Brown University you might not be surprised to learn that 95 percent of the student body earned As and Bs, but what about at a school like SUNY-Purchase, where 85 percent of the students recently received the same grades? The phenomenon is truly nationwide. Consider that in 1951, 21 percent of Penn State undergraduates earned As, compared with 44 percent more recently. At Furman University in South Carolina, 14 percent of students received As in 1951, compared with 41 percent today.[1]

Are students really getting that much smarter to justify rising GPAs? The short answer is no. But at the same time, I detect an increased sophistication among students today, who come to college better schooled in the study habits necessary to tackle college work. And really, if students have a basic complement of academic skills and are willing to put in considerable time—complete with visits to office hours and regular, early rough drafts of their papers—they ought to be able to earn at least Bs in college. Still, the larger truth is that it does not take as much today to do as well in college as it did when your parents, and especially your grandparents, attended college. I could fill an entire book with a tirade on grade inflation, and, certainly, many others have written about the perils of the problem.[2] But there is no point in ranting about the reality of college life today, and of course, you are not responsible for this phenomenon. Like generations before you, you've come to college with hopes for a successful education, and it's completely understandable that you want to do well. Grades are a measure of success, and they come with real-world consequences. Graduate school admission, fellowships and internships, and even prospective employment all can hinge on how well you have done in college. So even with the overall rise in student grades, your grades will matter.

• **As.** I suppose it's only fair to explain how I grade. It really depends on the class. In a course taught to a general student population, my grade distribution looks a lot broader than the numbers I just quoted above. It is difficult to get an A in my classes—and frankly it should be. Top grades are reserved for those students who, beyond understanding the basic terms of the class, are able to apply them. They also recognize the ramifications and limits of the concepts and can see broader applications or implications of the material. Almost invariably, they also write well. In my classes, 15–25 percent of the students would earn some form of an A.

• **Fs.** At the other end of the spectrum, few students ever fail my classes. I can count maybe twenty students who have failed out of more than a thousand I have taught over the years. Fs are reserved for students who don't even try. They refuse to do the reading, ditch class, and fail to take notes—usually all at the same time. These are the students who, by their actions, show that they don't want to be in college. They may tell me or even their parents that they like being a college student, but more often the answer is a cover for a student who appreciates the freedom of college without embracing the responsibility, or a student who is scared to tell a perceived authority figure that he would rather be doing something else. Remember, college is most certainly not for everyone, and there is no dishonor in trying college for a little while and then leaving to pursue stronger passions. If I could give these students any advice it would be to bite the bullet sooner rather than later. Maybe at a later time they will be ready and eager to attend college. But if their hearts and minds aren't in the enterprise, they should save the time and money for something better.

• **Ds.** Working our way back up the grading scale, Ds are often the dividing line between students who have what it takes to master college and those who do not. Generally, I find that D students fall into one of two camps, both of them disappointing in their own ways. At one end are the very bright students who just don't try. Oftentimes, these are the students who were smart enough in high school to skate by without doing the work. They score well on standardized tests, can bluff their way through an argument by using big words, and are used to passing a class by waiting until the last minute to read through the class material and then successfully wing it on an exam. They're so accustomed to this strategy from high school that they keep trying to replicate it in college. They choose frat parties over reading class material, go on road trips before big exams, and wait until the very last minute to write papers due the next day. But what they don't anticipate is that, unlike their high school teachers, their professors demand more in the way of breadth and depth of performance. It's not enough to spout big words on an exam if the argument that surrounds them doesn't relate to the material or answer the question. "Filling up space" has a long and notorious history in college papers, and any professor worth her salt can distinguish between a student who is applying the reading and another who is spouting drivel to meet a page limit. The latter often earn Ds for want of caring and effort.

The other group of Ds unfortunately comes from students who do not have the academic skills to tackle college-level material. Their writing is unsound—to the point of missing subject-verb agreements. They cannot keep up with the reading assignments even though they try, and they have trouble following the discussions in class. If you find yourself falling into this group, there are, fortunately, things you can do to help yourself. Many of these strategies are discussed in chapter 6.

Again, it is crucial that students recognize and address their problems as early as possible, because you want to avoid digging a hole for yourself so deep you can't escape. Experience tells me that most of these students are aware of their problems early in their college careers. The reading assignments seem to go on forever and are impenetrable, the lectures in class sound like they're in another language, and the many markings from the grammar check program make no sense. But rather than admitting their problems early in a class, they let them build up until, often with a just few weeks left in a semester, they appear on a professor's office doorstep asking for help. By then, however, it may be too late to pull out from the tailspin.

If you have any doubts about your academic skills, the best thing you can do for yourself is to bring them to someone's attention as early as possible in your college career. Talk to your academic advisor, take aside a sympathetic professor, or walk yourself over to the school's writing center and make an appointment. But whatever you do, ask for help, and ask early. There is not a reputable professor alive who wants to give a motivated student a bad grade because he lacks the academic skills to survive in a class. If you find yourself falling into this category, do what you can to address the problem.

• **Bs.** From where I sit, the big dividing line for student grades is in the B range. At one end of the spectrum, B+ students have just missed the A range, and at the other end, B− students have accomplished just enough to escape a C. A grade of B is a good, solid mark. It reflects that students understood the essence of what was taught and were even able to apply the concepts to related topics. Students who earn a B+ would even be described as performing very good work. What separates them from the A range is generally one of two issues. Some lack the writing skills to convey subtleties in their arguments. These students recognize the implications of the subjects covered but have difficulty explaining their arguments. The others can apply the concepts but only to a point. In a class on English literature, for example, they might recognize the writer's allusion to other works she has written but not to the political controversies of the day.

B– students, interestingly, also fall into similar camps. Some can explain their answers if asked to describe them orally but falter when faced with the prospect of writing. Others may be able to grasp the basic points of a course but have difficulty applying the lessons to other related issues. For example, they may understand the concept of prosecutorial discretion in a class on criminal justice but are unable to explain how sentencing guidelines give prosecutors even greater power because the charging decisions they make automatically set the range of acceptable sentences.

- **Cs.** Is the final remaining grade, a C, really that bad? Not in my world, where, routinely, one-quarter of a class may earn a C. But I recognize that for many students a C feels like failure, especially when so many of their classmates are earning higher grades. In my view, a C reflects a student's comprehension of the basic lessons of a class. In a course on evolutionary biology, for example, a student would understand and be able to explain how creatures evolved from earlier life forms into later animals. C students may not appreciate the subtlety of certain points or be able to apply the material consistently to hypothetical problems, but they have a command of the central points of the course and deserve their passing grades. Of course, if students are goofing off by failing to complete the reading, attend class, take notes, or prepare ahead for exams or papers, then that C is a mark of how they did not ready themselves. But a student who is giving it her all and achieves a C has my respect.

You Are Not Your Grades

Before I leave the subject of grading, let me offer you two cautions. More and more, I see students who envision their grades as a measure of their self-worth. It really pains me to see this, even if I understand its origins.

In today's hyper-competitive world, parents and schools start early in preparing students for college. Undoubtedly, you were encouraged to earn top marks in high school in order to be accepted to the college of your choice. Some of you may never have earned a C, and I suspect there are some of you who would even view a B as a mark of failure. I know it's really hard to break yourself from this mold, especially when it seems like the world around you is pushing for high grades, but you're well on the way to a life of insecurity and self-doubt if you equate your self-worth with your GPA.

Eventually, what will get you up out of bed each morning, what will give you a sense of satisfaction at the end of the day, is whether you have done what you enjoy, whether you have had a chance to interact with people you like and admire and who feel the same way about you. Sure, particular jobs may require good grades, but the most successful graduates I have known are those who took a small opportunity and sought to make the most of it. They didn't rely on their transcripts for this, because—let me assure you—by the time you reach your second job no one will care what your GPA was in college. Employers will want to know if you show up on time, do what you say you will, treat others well, and provide more value to the organization than you take from it. Some of those skills are also predictors of good grades, but the reverse is most certainly not true. A high GPA is not a guarantee of professional success.

Don't Be a Grade Grubber

Even if you're not yet thinking of your days after graduation—and, really, you don't need to start planning for that until you are further into your college career—the mindless pursuit of grades is dangerous to you on a more immediate level: it is a big turnoff for faculty. If you want to annoy your instructor, spend as much time as you can throughout the semester asking, "Will this affect my grade?" "How many points will I earn from the extra credit assignment?" and "Why did I only get half credit for this answer?" Professors value students who are interested in learning, who recognize that grades are a mark of student performance but not the primary goal of education, and who approach their instructors respectfully rather than accusatorially when questioning particular marks.

If your focus is on grades for grades' sake, if you are seen as constantly pushing for every little advantage in grading, you are essentially telling your professor that you are not serious about learning. Although I cannot prove it, I would bet that perceived "grade grubbers" usually fail to get the benefit of the doubt when their final grade falls on the cusp. Students might expect the opposite, figuring that by constantly hounding their professors for better grades, the instructors would eventually accede, if only because the teachers would recognize how important the higher grades are to the students. But the opposite is more likely true. Students who seem to disrespect the educational process by their overemphasis on perceived output measures mistake the real output that professors seek—understanding, which itself is achieved by student interest and effort in learning. There is no mistaking that grading is important. All I'm asking you to do is to keep it in perspective.

Why Professors Conduct Tests

If you were to ask a group of professors whether they enjoyed conducting examinations, the answer would likely be mixed. On one hand, there are some instructors who enjoy the proverbial process of "separating the wheat from the chaff." They want to see their better students rewarded for hard work and may take a little perverse pleasure in the prospect of students who have blown off the course enduring the consequences. In addition, professors are always reassured by results that show their students have learned the material, which in several ways is a reflection of the instructor's ability to teach. But at the same time, most true teachers detest anything that removes the focus of the class from the learning process and redirects it to the angst of scores and grades. I even know of one professor who refuses to assign a test during her course because she believes exams "spoil the nurturing atmosphere of the classroom." She, however, is an exception. So long as a course requires an evaluation of student work, so long as there are grades, professors are going to employ examinations.

Different Kinds of Tests

I have been talking about exams as if they all follow a similar structure, but in reality there are different kinds of tests. Some are closed book while others permit students to rely on their notes. Some are timed, others are not. Some even last for an entire week as a take-home assignment. In general, though, faculty tend to rely on five kinds of examinations: 1) quizzes; 2) multiple-choice or true-false; 3) short-answer; 4) essays; and 5) take-home.

Quizzes are similar to what you likely took in high school and are usually designed to make sure that students have been keeping up with the reading or paying attention in lecture. Quizzes may be as short as five questions or as long as twenty-five, but they generally follow the same format. The danger for students, however, is that many quizzes are offered without notice—the proverbial pop quiz—so you won't know when to prepare for them other than keeping up with the reading and attending class.

Multiple-choice and true-false exams are what you're undoubtedly familiar with from your many years of standardized testing. Each question presents you with a statement and two to five answers from which to choose. Depending on the time set aside for the exam and the difficulty of the questions, multiple-choice exams can be as short as twenty-five questions or as long as several hundred.

Short-answer exams are a cross between multiple-choice and the essay tests around which many of your upper-level classes are built. In a short-answer exam, students are asked a variety of questions and provided a relatively small space—two or three lines—in which to write their answers. The idea of a short-answer exam is to challenge the student to say something incisive about the material by going beyond rote repetition without asking him to write a longer analytical piece.

Essay and take-home exams operate on a shared principle. They require students to step back from the material, construct an argument, and present this position in several pages of prose. Essay exams may be open or closed book (referring to which resources, if any, students are permitted to consult during an exam). In an open-book test, students may bring their notes and examine any of the readings from the course while constructing their answers. In closed-book exams, students are not permitted to consult anything but their memories.

Invariably, students believe that closed-book exams will be more difficult. But in reality, faculty expect more of students on open-book exams, where the emphasis is not on the facts that students have remembered about the subject but how persuasively they can apply the concepts from the class. Almost by definition, take-home exams are open book, since students typically are assigned the exam in a class session and then permitted up to a week to complete the test at home.

Given the almost irresistible temptation to consult one's notes outside of the classroom, faculty generally permit students to utilize anything they have read or created in the class for the purposes of completing a take-home exam.

Tests and Learning Objectives

To some extent, a professor's choice of exam reflects her learning goals for the class. Most professors are familiar with something called the "taxonomy of teaching objectives," which Benjamin Bloom, a famous educational psychologist, and colleagues created in the 1950s.[3] According to Bloom, there are successive levels of student learning, which can be ranked by increasing depths of analytical thought. Educators have since updated Bloom's taxonomy, to the point that many professors would now describe these levels of learning as such:[4]

Remembering: Recalling facts, terms, and principles

Understanding: Comprehending and explaining material

Applying: Using a concept to solve a problem

Analyzing: Recognizing how parts relate to each other and overall structure

Evaluating: Assessing and critiquing ideas using specific criteria

Creating: Integrating ideas into a new conception

Updated Bloom's taxonomy of levels of learning

For example, in a class on American history, a remembering goal would ask students to recall important dates, such as 1776, when the Declaration of Independence was written, or 1787, when the Constitution was ratified. An understanding goal would seek to have students explain the importance of material, such as understanding the significance of the Declaration of Independence as the colonists' official break from England and King George III. An application goal would encourage students to employ their understanding of the course material to solve a related problem. In the same history class, then, students might be asked to apply the thinking of James Madison to a contemporary issue of politics or policy. An analyzing goal would encourage students to link different concepts together, such as being able to explain which forces led the colonists to revolt. An evaluation goal would ask students to critique the material they had just covered. Here, students might be asked to compare the relative arguments of the colonies and King George and evaluate who had the better grievance. Finally, a creation goal would expect students to take what they had learned and create an original work of their own. Keeping with the history example, an instructor might ask students to write a response to the Declaration of Independence based on the political philosophy of those colonists loyal to the king.

Generally, introductory classes demand lower-level learning objectives, while advanced courses require deeper thinking. In a first-semester chemistry class, for example, instructors often are content if students can recall the periodic table, whereas by the time students reach upper-level courses, they are expected to conduct their own experiments to test hypotheses about the interactions of particular substances. This does not mean that first-year classes are necessarily "easier" than upper-level classes, for it can be difficult to comprehend a new subject with its unique terminology and concepts; rather, the differences reflect the natural learning curve of a new subject.

If you ever learned to sail, you know that you first had to learn the parts of a boat (remembering) and grasp the principle of wind direction (understanding) before you were turned loose to trim the sails and steer the boat (applying and creating). The same is true in your college classes. For example, an introductory class in macroeconomics first familiarizes students with the elements of the demand curve before upper-level classes encourage students to estimate the effects of a tax cut on the national economy.

Multiple-Choice and True-False Exams

Given the nature of introductory classes, it is not surprising that exams in these courses employ testing formats generally designed to showcase basic knowledge and comprehension. Multiple-choice or true-false questions typically ask students to apply the definitions of subjects or explain the basic meaning of a concept. By contrast, once students learn the essential terminology of a discipline, more advanced classes will ask them to apply, synthesize, and evaluate related issues through exams that increasingly rely on essays or problem solving.

These are not, however, ironclad rules, for even multiple-choice exams can be employed to test students' abilities to analyze or evaluate the course material. Here, I'm indebted to biology professor Michael Tansey and his colleagues at Indiana University, for illustrative examples of multiple-choice questions.[5] As I've said, multiple-choice questions are usually employed to test students' basic knowledge, and Tansey offers a classic example. In an introductory course on cell biology, he might ask:

1. Which of the following are the raw materials for photosynthesis?
   a. Water, heat, sunlight
   b. Carbon dioxide, sunlight, oxygen
   c. Water, carbon dioxide, sunlight
   d. Sunlight, oxygen, carbohydrates
   e. Water, carbon dioxide, carbohydrates

A question like this essentially tests students' knowledge of the definition of a concept. But multiple-choice questions can be employed for more advanced thinking, like this example from Tansey that asks students to synthesize and evaluate the concepts associated with a subject:

2. Mitochondria are called the powerhouses of the cell because they make energy available for cellular metabolism. Which of the following observations is most convincing in explaining this concept of mitochondrial function?
   a. ATP occurs in the mitochondria.
   b. Mitochondria have a double membrane.
   c. The enzymes of the Krebs cycle and molecules required for terminal respiration are found in mitochondria.
   d. Mitochondria are found in almost all kinds of plant and animal cells.
   e. Mitochondria abound in muscle tissue.

Advantages and Disadvantages of These Exams

There are several reasons that an instructor might employ a multiple-choice or true-false exam. The versatility of multiple questions permits a professor to cover many concepts and levels of comprehension. Students cannot "bluff" an answer or "write around" the question if they do not know the material.[6] And because the answers are objectively scored, grading is rarely open to charges of variability or favoritism. Still, I am not a fan of multiple-choice exams. All too often, professors employ these formats out of laziness. Although a multiple-choice exam can be time-consuming to write, it is simple to grade. At campuses that have Scantron machines, answer sheets can be mechanically scored and the grades computed relatively quickly. In a class of two hundred-plus students, the prospect of hand grading stacks of blue books can be daunting, and for this reason professors may turn to multiple-choice or true-false exams where grading can be done, literally, with the push of a button. Plus, a good multiple-choice exam can be used in future classes (although hopefully modified somewhat so that students cannot predict all of the questions from past exams).

From a student's perspective, multiple-choice exams do not allow partial credit: an answer is either right or wrong, and a student who has good ideas but misses one link in his thinking is denied any credit. For that matter, multiple-choice exams do not promote effective writing. From my own experience, I can say that college students do not get enough practice in argumentative or expository writing, some of the most important "real-world" skills that we can possibly teach. Once you leave college and take that first job, you will be expected to communicate your ideas and conclusions to others, and you won't have the luxury of spending two weeks polishing a draft. If there is any place to hone these skills, it is in college, and if there is any environment in which to give you practice in the skills of writing under time pressure, then it is an exam. For these reasons, I and many of my colleagues rely on essay, or blue book, exams, especially in classes above the introductory level.

Essay Exams

Blue book exams get their name from the color of the covers of the booklets that students use to write their answers. These exams generally entail two to five questions, some even with multiple parts. Rather than relying on simple recall or comprehension, essay tests focus on the more advanced levels of learning. Students are asked to analyze, evaluate, and apply ideas from the course, and in some cases, they are required to create a new work, such as a poem, a letter, or a theory.

There are many kinds of essay questions. Here is an example of one I gave on an exam. In a class titled Law and Society, I wanted to assess the students' abilities to apply the readings to critique the American legal system. In this essay, students were expected to know those readings, understand what the authors' arguments were, apply them to an evaluative question, and then stake out their own position:

> *Imagine that you have just graduated and found work at a research institute. There you are assigned to a senior researcher, who tells you:*
>
>> *Everyone always thinks that law advances rights, but I believe that law limits freedom. I'm going to write a journal article that makes this argument, but I'm not sure what examples I can use to make my case. Since you have recently completed a class on law and society, you must have some ideas. How can I support this argument? What readings from your class help to advance this claim?*
>>
>> *I want this article to be a strong as possible, so please lay out for me the counterarguments that I must address. Can you summarize the readings that make the best case against my position?*
>>
>> *Finally, since you're a smart person, I'm interested in your own perspective. Do you agree with my position, or do you think I'm wrong? Why?*
>
> *The senior researcher asks that you write her a memorandum answering these many questions. Please be as thorough and detailed in your response as possible.*

The beauty of a question like this is that there isn't a single "right" answer. Rather, the best answers are those in which students are able to stake out a position; apply the readings, lectures, and class discussions to their analysis; and consider and respond to alternative perspectives. Later in this chapter I will walk you through effective strategies for answering essay exams. For now, however, my goal is to introduce you to the format and purpose of essay tests.

The best professors I know prefer essay exams and the analytical thinking they require. Essay tests typically focus students' attention on broader understandings of course material, and they present students with a more realistic—and, admittedly, demanding!—task than merely choosing between multiple answers. But essay exams also have their limits. They cover less material, they take much more time to grade, and their scoring is less objective than multiple-choice tests.

Preparing for an Exam

So enough about the theory of exams. You undoubtedly want to know how to prepare for them. Fortunately, if you have been attending class, taking notes, and keeping up with the reading and any homework assignments, you're a long way toward being ready for the test. Perhaps the first task is to recognize what material will be covered on the exam. If it's a quiz you're facing, then the scope of the examination will likely be narrow. In all likelihood, the professor is interested in seeing if you have been doing the reading and have grasped the concepts there. By contrast, a midterm examination likely will include anything you have gone over from the beginning of the class to that point in the semester. Final exams can be tricky, and you need to clarify with your professor what material is fair game for the test. In many classes, the final covers material presented throughout the semester, but some professors only test on material covered since the midterm. By talking with your instructor ahead of time, you will be able to focus your studying on those subjects that will be covered on the exam.

Regardless of the scope of material to be tested, the process of studying for an exam should be relatively similar. You need to do at least two things, and ideally a third: 1) go back over the reading and your class notes to clarify any issues you did not fully understand at the time; 2) synthesize those notes and reading into your own study guide; and 3) if you want to cover all your bases, practice answering possible exam questions, especially if the test is a final exam. These steps are essential and should become your routine. Yet I see too many students who do not appreciate how to study for an exam. They seem to believe that if they simply review the reading and look over their class notes a few times, they'll be set. But that kind of studying only helps students memorize material. If you want to be able to apply, analyze, or evaluate the course material on an exam, then you have to practice doing that with "active studying."

Step 1—Clarify

As I said, your first task in studying should be to clarify any questions you had when the course material was presented in class. Let's say your philosophy professor was discussing the writings of John Stuart Mill and had been explaining the implications of Mill's theory of utilitarianism. Looking back through your notes, do you understand what that theory was and could you apply it to a current political debate? If not, return to the assigned reading and see if you can find the answer in there. If not, or even as a supplement, go to office hours to see if your professor can clear up your confusion.

Step 2—Study Guide

Once you have resolved any obvious confusion about the material, start creating a study guide. Essentially, a study guide is a truncated version of your class notes and highlighted reading assignments that will help you to summarize the material covered in the course. Some study guides are long—I've seen upwards of twenty pages for a final exam in a complicated class—but many are four to five pages. The key is to highlight the obvious issues covered in the course to date by writing down dates, terminology, or people you are supposed to know; summarizing ideas, concepts, or theories addressed; and noting connections between those themes. Essentially, the study guide should help you remember and understand the material covered and offer criteria that might be applied in analyzing or evaluating the course content.

Students sometimes ask me, "How do I distinguish the important ideas to cover from those that are more minor?" This can be a difficult process, especially for students who are used to taking notes on anything and everything a professor utters, but there are some rules that can help you to focus your studying. In preparing for an exam, begin with the readings and make sure that you understand any terms that are highlighted in the books or articles. If your instructor has assigned a textbook, the summaries at chapter end usually highlight the most important terms and concepts covered. But more than anything, go through your class notes to see what your instructor said in class, because that's where you are likely to find hints—some even quite deliberate suggestions—about what you are expected to master. In particular, pay special attention to anything:

- the instructor said would be on the test.
- the instructor repeatedly emphasized in class.
- the instructor said he or she especially cared about.
- the instructor and readings both covered.

A study guide is a wonderful start in preparing for a test, and in truth, simply memorizing it may be enough to succeed in a class in which the instructor merely wishes students to remember and repeat back the course content. In such a class, studying by flash cards or crafting a mnemonic list may be the way to go. For example, if you are trying to remember the order of the visible color spectrum—red, orange, yellow, green, blue, indigo, violet—you might create the sentence "**R**ebecca **O**penly **Y**ells '**G**o **B**lue' **I**n **V**ictory" to help you keep track of the list. In this case, the first letter of each word in the sentence corresponds to the first letter of each color in order. As odd as this technique may seem, it is quite effective. The trick is to pick an expression that means something to you. In my case, can you figure out my undergraduate alma mater?

Step 3—Practice Exams

Any professor worth his salt, however, will want students to go beyond memorization to apply, evaluate, and analyze the material. This is where it's important to practice those skills, a task that can be done by creating and answering mock test questions. How much time you spend on this will depend upon the significance of the exam. If you're studying for a test on just two chapters of a book, it's not necessary to practice possible exam answers. But if the exam is a final, then you ought to put in the time. You might consider studying with a group so that members can take turns crafting sample questions for the others to try answering. At first, the answers need not be written out. Simply outlining an answer will help you compose a response, which you should share with others in the group for useful feedback. As the test gets closer, though, you should attempt a dry run by writing out an answer so that you have a sense of how long it takes you to plan and fully answer a question.

In addition to consulting your classmates over sample answers, you should look for past exams in the class, as these will provide an excellent guide of what the professor is likely to ask. If you cannot find a past exam, approach the instructor directly for some help in thinking through possible questions. Although most professors will not provide sample questions, they should be willing to evaluate any mock questions you create on your own. If you're fortunate, they will meet with you ahead of the test to give you a sense of how well you answered your model questions. If you are willing to put in this kind of time, you are almost assured of doing well on the exam. This is true whether the test is essay or multiple-choice, as practicing model questions with your instructor's feedback is the single best way of understanding what is likely to be on a test and being ready to do your best.

Staying on Top of the Material

If you have been keeping up on your reading, adding notes in the margins, attending class, and taking useful notes, then you will be in good shape to study for an exam. Prepared like this, you would only need a couple of days to get ready for a midterm exam. For a final, the preparation process needs to start sooner, as you have more material to cover. Obviously, the less attention you have paid to the reading or the fewer classes you have attended and notes taken, the longer you will need to catch up before you can prepare for an exam. That's why I recommend crafting your study guide as you go throughout the term. After each major subject in the class is discussed, take a little time to summarize what was covered in the readings and in class. This can be done every couple of weeks or even weekly to get yourself in the habit of staying prepared. I can tell you—alas, from my own experience as an undergraduate— that there is no fun in the panic at semester's end when you're working furiously to summarize a really complicated class. Make preparation a regular practice.

That said, if exam day dawns and you're still not confident that you know the material, then you need both to console yourself and muster the best attitude you can for test taking. Rather than focusing on what you don't know, tell yourself that you will do your best and that you assuredly know much more than you do not. Don't psych yourself out by going into the test with extreme self-doubt.

Why Are You Doing This?

If it seems like I am offering you some "secret of success" for test taking, it may naturally raise the question why more students don't ace their exams. The simple answer is that the vast majority of students don't put in this kind of preparation for an exam. Some are scared of approaching their instructors, especially if they fear appearing "wrong" as they are learning the material. Others aren't used to this kind of studying from high school or are unaware that past exams generally float around college campuses as freely as the air everyone breathes. But still more aren't prepared to make this kind of commitment to their classes. Even as I wish they would, I understand why they don't. This kind of preparation is time-consuming. It takes you away from extracurricular activities, work, and socializing. But it's necessary. No matter how you study in college, it is likely to be longer than you did in high school, probably by 50 percent at least. The goal here is not simply to ace your classes (although that is a nice side benefit). The ultimate reason is to feel that you have mastered and can apply the education you have received.

Yes, I know that sounds achingly idealist and perhaps naive. But if you're going to spend all this time and money at college, shouldn't you actually learn the material you're being taught? And by learn, I mean more than simply regurgitating the content back on a test. True education is an active process that requires the involvement of the student. If you want to actually understand what you have been taught, to be able to apply it in ways that will make your life more interesting and your future professional life more successful, then you need to take the time in college to reinforce and expand on what you are told in the classroom or read in your textbooks. That is where the studying process comes into play. You have to take what you have been given and make it your own.

Where to Study

As a veteran student, you are likely familiar with the advice to study in a spot with few distractions. Certainly, research suggests that students retain more information if they are not inundated with lots of other stimuli while learning or studying.[7] But distraction means different things to different people. I have seen plenty of students who need the noise of a cafe around them to feel in the mood to study, just as I know lots of students who cannot concentrate unless they are wearing earplugs. The key here is discovering the environment you need to be able to focus. Those students who can study amidst seeming chaos are able to block out external stimuli and, more remarkably, seem best able to do so when their ears are being bombarded with outside noise. In a sense, they are hyper-focused.

The same does not extend to those students who try to focus on several things at once. You know them; perhaps you're one yourself—the students who listen to their iPods while surfing the Internet with the television on behind them as they look back and forth at their math notebook. These students assuredly are not learning the material as well as they would if they simply put their attention on the task at hand. Indeed, most research to date suggests that we are fooling ourselves if we think we're able to multitask. Rather than focusing on several things at once, studies show that our brains are actually shifting focus in rapid-fire succession between the many stimuli.[8] So whether you prefer the quiet of the library or the noise of your dorm, try to limit yourself to doing one thing at a time.

The Night Before

There are a number of test taking strategies that apply to a variety of exams. Regardless of whether you are preparing for a quiz or a final, you ought to follow many of the same strategies regardless of the test's form to make the process less stressful and give yourself the greatest chance of success. First is getting enough sleep. There are reams of studies that show sleep deprivation hinders student performance on tests,[9] and yet finals week routinely finds students pulling all-nighters to try to study for exams. I'm under no illusion that the practice will magically stop, especially when students are learning to balance the responsibilities of studying against the allure of an active social life and other distractions in college. But even so, I need to emphasize how important a good night's sleep is.

Plan your sleep at least two nights in advance of your exam. Even if you find yourself anxious on the night before a big test, the sleep you built up ahead of time should help to carry you through the exam. The night before an exam, turn off your phone and do something that is enjoyable for you—within reason. That trip to the bars or the blowout party at the frat house needs to wait until you've finished your tests. But in the meantime, find something that you enjoy that will have you in bed at a reasonable hour. Speaking of bed, you may want to take a look at your notes one last time before turning out the lights, since research shows that material reviewed before bedtime is likely to stay with you.[10] But by review, I mean take a short glance. Your goal should be simply to refresh your memory, not create anxiety immediately before you go to sleep.

I hope it goes without saying that you need to set an alarm the morning of your exam if the test will be given early in the day. If you're an especially deep sleeper or if you are worried about sleeping through your exam, set two alarms or make a pact with someone else in your class to check on each other in the morning to confirm that you're both awake. To repeat what your parents have undoubtedly told you over the years, make sure you have a good breakfast, or, if the test is later in the day, eat something before the exam so that you are well fueled. Go easy on the caffeine or Red Bull, though. Research suggests its effects are temporary, but the resulting anxiety can keep you from concentrating on the test.[11]

On the night before your test, double-check the rules the professor has set for what you may—and may not—bring with you. If you must provide blue books for your essay answers or Scantron forms for multiple-choice tests, make sure you purchase these ahead of time, along with sufficient pens or pencils. Try to plan for the worst—like your pen exploding, the person next to you spilling water on one of your blue books, and the like—and bring extras. If for some reason your professor permits you to answer your exam by computer (a rarity, for fear that students will show up at the exam with canned answers already saved in their hard drives), then make sure your computer's battery is fully charged and remember to bring the electrical cord as well. If the professor has prohibited cell phones, iPods, or even hats (more on cheating in a moment), keep them stowed away in your backpack and be prepared to check them with a proctor as you enter the exam room. If you are taking a final, your professor may permit you to bring a snack to eat over what may be a three-hour exam. But again, make sure you know what the restrictions are for the goodies you bring with you. I know instructors who insist on examining the packaging of snacks to ensure that students have not tried to hide notes on the sides.

Exam Day

Leave yourself enough time to get to the exam. If you're reliant on a campus bus or are at the mercy of local traffic to get to school, add 50 percent to your commute time. Unless there is a horrific storm, fire, or earthquake that impedes travel (without somehow also canceling the exam), your teacher is unlikely to be sympathetic or offer extra time to complete the test. Also build in additional time to go to the bathroom before the exam, especially if you have a nervous bladder. I've seen plenty of anxious students lose time on an exam because they have had to go use the facilities. If you can get by without leaving to get a drink or go to the bathroom, forego the visit unless you really need the chance to step out and you're on pace to finish the exam well before the deadline. Also keep in mind that some professors won't allow "pee breaks" during exams.

I generally recommend that students get to the exam room early and stake out a seat. For some exams, you will be assigned a seat by the instructor as a way of preventing cheating. But where you are permitted to choose your seat, jump at the chance. Just as in an airplane, you might be able to snag a seat on the aisle, one that allows you to answer questions without being bumped on your writing elbow. By arriving early, you'll also get one more chance to look over your study sheet. Don't be a slave to the sheet, though, desperately trying to memorize it. The time for serious study already has passed. Instead, you may want to take a moment or two to refresh your memory and keep the concepts upfront in your short-term memory. (Ideally, by then you will have cemented the concepts in your long-term memory as well.) Try visualizing yourself answering the questions as you hope to do. Part of doing well on an exam is coming into it with a calm and confident attitude. Try some relaxation exercises; deep breathing, closing your eyes, and tensing then releasing various muscle groups may help you to keep your anxiety in check. Try to keep the whole experience in perspective. If the test is anything other than a final exam, a bad grade can be overcome in other ways, and even a bombed final is not terminal. This is one exam in one class over the course of your entire life. Don't overreact.

Previewing the Exam

Once the exam is handed out, spend several minutes reading the directions carefully. You would be surprised by how many students lose precious points on an exam because they skipped the directions. Then scan through the questions to see how many there are and what types are being employed. It is essential that you pace yourself. If, for example, you have fifty minutes to answer a hundred multiple-choice questions, you know that, on average, you have no more than two minutes per question to make up your mind. But approach this even more conservatively. Set aside upwards of ten minutes as a reserve, both to go back and double-check your answers and also as a safety net in case you begin to fall behind in completing the test. If the exam consists of essays, take a close look at how grading is assigned. If one question is worth twice as many points as another, you should concentrate a greater percentage of your time on the more prominent question. Don't fall into the habit of spending so much time on your first essay that you don't have enough time to devote to other questions. You can avoid this by setting deadlines for yourself, marking the times on your blue book at which you must stop answering each question based on their proportional values.

Let's try a concrete example. Imagine that your professor has assigned three essay questions to answer over seventy minutes, with their values set at 25 percent, 25 percent, and 50 percent of the exam grade, respectively. If you reserved ten minutes to go back and read over your essays at the end of the exam, you would have sixty minutes for the essays. Ideally, then, you should spend fifteen minutes answering each of the first two questions and thirty minutes responding to the third based on their proportional values. So if your professor hands out the exam at 10:00 a.m., you would write "10:15" next to question one, to remind yourself that you must move on to the next question at that point, and "10:30" by question two so that you would know you needed to move on to the final question by then. Finishing question three at 11:00, you would still have ten minutes to go back over your answers and incorporate any edits before time is up.

Of course, the example above presumes that you would choose to answer the questions in order, which I do not recommend. Instead, as soon as the exam is handed out, briefly look over the questions and make a mental note of which ones seem easier for you. Start with these. Among other things, you're likely to get through these questions at a faster pace than you have allotted, which will give you confidence, and you can then concentrate your energies on those questions that are more difficult for you. But unless you are running ahead of the time you have allotted for each question, do not linger. Acing one question while giving the others short shrift will almost always end in a mediocre grade for the exam.

If the exam is multiple-choice, don't bother previewing the questions. Instead, complete the easy questions quickly, passing over any questions about which you have doubts on a first reading. Once you have gotten the easy questions out of the way, count up the number of hard questions remaining and look at the amount of time you have left. Set yourself a time limit for each question, and then go through the difficult questions in order, making sure that you move on whenever the time for answering each expires. If you set aside a little extra time for yourself at the end of the exam, you can go back and think through the trickiest questions before you must turn in the answer sheet. In fact, you might consider making marks on the questions (but not the answer sheet) as you answer them, signifying which answers you're sure are correct and which other ones you should go back and review with your extra time.

How to Answer Multiple-Choice Exams

One of the skills that often distinguishes the best test takers from others is the ability to appreciate what is being asked in the questions. Certainly, if the exam is true-false or multiple-choice, the mechanics of answering questions is relatively easy: you simply need to check a box, circle an answer, or fill in an oval. But be careful that you don't trip over particular words in the question. If a true-false query uses the words "always" or "never," note that you're being asked whether there are *any* exceptions that might negate the statement presented. If a multiple-choice question offers options that include "all of the above" or "none of the above" the instructor wants to know if you understand the definition of a concept and which elements are included. When you look at a multiple-choice question, see if you can answer it before even peeking at the choices. If you know the answer and find it among the options, then fill in the answer sheet and cross off the question on the test sheet as one you're sure you answered correctly.

If you're uncertain of a question or you see more than one option that seems plausible among the possible answers, then imagine that you need to explain your answer to the professor. If you can justify one option more than the others, then that is your answer. Mark the answer sheet and move on. If you come back to the question later, resist the urge to change your answer unless, upon further reflection, you are certain you have a better argument to justify your choice. Too often, students second-guess themselves on an answer when in fact their first instinct is more often correct. If you are truly unsure of a question, eliminate those options you know to be incorrect, leave the question unanswered, then come back to it near the end of the exam to see if you have a new perspective on the question.

Perhaps the hardest multiple-choice questions are those that ask "which of these statements best describes" a concept or theme. In cases like these, the professor is testing your ability to evaluate the relative worth of particular arguments. On a question like this, usually two or three answers will have a kernel of truth, and you'll be forced to deduce which one is most sensible. The problem is that you cannot get partial credit for your response, even if your logic is mostly correct. This is one of the reasons that I do not like multiple-choice questions—they stifle, or at least limit, analytical reasoning. To give yourself the best chance on questions like these, put yourself through the paces of defending your logic, perhaps even sketching out your reasoning next to the test question. That way, even if you get the question wrong, you'll have some proof of your thinking if you want to argue later that the question was vague or had more than one correct answer.

I presume it goes without saying that there is no way to gain partial credit on a true-false or multiple-choice exam. You either have left yourself enough time to answer all of the questions or you have not. But unlike some standardized tests, there is nothing to be gained by leaving an answer blank even if you do not know the correct response. If the question is true-false, you have a 50 percent chance of getting the answer correct by guessing; in a multiple-choice exam, the odds drop to 20 or 25 percent for a guess, but either is certainly higher than 0, which is what you will earn by leaving an answer blank. Make sure you answer every question—even better, avoid this dilemma by planning your time well.

How to Answer Essay Exams

When facing an essay test, the most important skill is recognizing what you're being asked to do in your answer. Here, there are several terms that can tip you off to what's expected in a test question. If you'll recall the six levels of cognitive thought, there are key words in test questions that will let you know what type of response is required. These are described in the table below.

Applying six levels of cognitive thought in essay exams

Cognitive level	Student activity	Words to look for in questions
Remembering	recalling facts, terms, concepts, definitions, and principles	define, identify, label, list, name, state
Understanding	explaining or interpreting the meaning of material	account for, convert, explain, give an example, infer, interpret, paraphrase, predict, summarize, translate
Applying	using a concept or principle to solve a problem	apply, compute, demonstrate, make use of, modify, show, solve
Analyzing	recognizing how parts relate to each other and the overall structure	break down, connect, correlate, dissect, explore, relate, link
Evaluating	making a judgment based on a preestablished set of criteria	appraise, critique, evaluate, judge, justify, recommend, which would be better
Creating	producing something new or original from component parts	change, construct, create, design, develop, formulate, imagine, write a dialogue or short story

Source: Lucy C. Jacobs, "How to Write Better Tests: A Handbook for Improving Test Construction Skills," IUB Evaluation Services & Testing, accessed December 23, 2010, http://www.indiana.edu/~best/write_better_tests.shtml.

If you get used to scrutinizing the words in your test questions, you will be that much further ahead in understanding what skills are at play. Suppose a test question asks you to explain why the dinosaurs became extinct. Taking a quick look at the chart above, you would recognize that your instructor is testing your understanding or comprehension of a topic. You need not evaluate the effects of extinction or produce your own theory; rather, you are being asked to recount the explanation offered in class or the readings. By contrast, if the question asks you to appraise the effects of the dinosaurs' extinction, then simply describing the process of their disappearance would fail to address the question's focus on evaluation. Tailoring your answer to the specific question is an important skill, for your professors are undoubtedly (and unfortunately) all too accustomed to the student answer that seems to throw everything against the proverbial wall in hope that an important kernel or two sticks. Believe me, your instructors can recognize when you know the answer to a question and when you're blowing smoke, hoping that they'll give you credit for showing something—anything—that you know. But just as voters dislike politicians who fail to answer reporters' questions in favor of espousing their talking points, professors grade down answers that don't address the issue asked and instead attempt to show everything that a student claims to know about a topic.

In addition to focusing on the specific question asked, the best essay answers have at least three things in common. First, they are well organized. Students have taken time to outline an answer that shows a logical, easily followed train of thought. Second, students cite to the readings, lectures, or class discussions to support their points. There is no better way to demonstrate that you have completed and comprehended the reading than to cite key points from the assignments when answering a question. Third, students fully explain their points. It is not enough simply to state a position; a good essay also provides a basis for the conclusion.

Surprisingly, students know this in other parts of their lives, but they mysteriously seem to forget the approach when in class, especially when taking an exam. Think of the last time you had an argument with someone over sports. My editor and I do this all the time over Chicago baseball teams. We could stand at six paces and mindlessly shout "Cubs" or "White Sox" at each other, but this would hardly convince anyone that we were correct. Instead, the more convincing approach would be to marshal facts—examining team history, beauty of the stadium, fervor of the fans, and yes (reluctantly for this Cubs fan), player statistics—to explain why it is better to root for one team over the other.

The same is true on an exam. If you're being asked to evaluate which theory of political philosophy best preserves individual liberty in modern-day America, your professor expects you to stake out a position and marshal the facts from the readings and class discussions to explain your position. But even more, consider alternative arguments that challenge your position and respond to them explaining why, nonetheless, your position is the more reasonable view. These last two skills truly distinguish the best exams. By necessity, a student who recognizes the limits of her position and is able to address them is explaining the merits of her answer. If she grounds her explanations in the readings and class discussions, she has done all she can to excel on the exam.

If You Run Out of Time

On the off chance that you run out of time on an essay exam, it's important to show as much of you work as possible, even if you are unable to write it all down. This is why (among other reasons) it's so essential to craft an outline for your answers before you begin writing. Put these on the inside cover of your blue book or on the first few pages so you can always refer your instructor to the outlines if you need to show her what you were planning to write. Even if you don't use an outline, make it easy for your professor to understand your argument by employing a definitive structure in your answers. In the first paragraph of the answer, tell her what your overall conclusion will be and note the arguments you will make. Of course, you will be better off if you have planned sufficient time to answer the exam questions completely; but even if you have not, an outline and structured opening paragraph will allow your instructor to appreciate that you understood the course material and have interesting points to make as a result.

After the Test Is Over

If your class is like many others, there usually will be one student who turns in his exam well ahead of his classmates. If your course is a large class, I can almost guarantee it. You'll be working away on your test, keeping to your time limits on each question, when you'll catch movement out of the corner of your eye and see a student stride up to the podium ready to turn in his exam even as the clock shows one-third of the allotted time still remaining. It's easy to panic in that situation, but do not. Resist the voice of self doubt that begins asking, "How did he finish this test so easily while I'm still slaving away? If he could answer the questions so quickly, I have no chance of a good grade." Actually, it's likely just the opposite, for the student who finishes so far ahead of the rest of the class usually does not know the material.

Think about it for a moment. If the test is an essay exam, how much faster could you finish if you had nothing to say to the questions? Or, in a multiple-choice test, what is there to agonize over in choosing answers if none of the options reads better than the others? So long as you are not rushing at the end, frantically trying to cram everything you know about a question into the five remaining minutes, you should not be worried about when in the pack you finish. Students answer questions at their own pace. In fact, my best students over the years have been the ones who wait until the end of the test period to turn in their exams, having made sure that they used all of the allotted time to go back over and double-check their responses.

I know I'm likely sounding like your parents. How many times in your childhood did you hear the expression, "the only person you need to compare yourself to is you?" But if this sounds like a platitude, it's only because it is true. Once you turn in your exam, avoid at all costs the impulse to compare answers with your classmates. I see this all the time. Out in the hall there is a gaggle of nervous students anxiously going over the test. "What did you write for question ten? It was Edith Wharton, right?" There is nothing to be gained by these discussions unless you like self-inflicted torture. Inevitably, the students clumped together will disagree about the correct result, thus providing no relief from their anxiety, or a group of them will confirm that they answered a question the same way, which will turn out later to have been incorrect.

Once the test is over, it's done. No manner of kibitzing or worrying will change your answers or result, and in fact, continuing to obsess about the test will only feed your anxiety. If you have studied effectively for the exam, then you likely have done well. Perhaps not exceptionally, and certainly not perfectly, but well just the same. So have the self-confidence—and most importantly, the self-preservation instinct—to put the exam to bed metaphorically in your mind. Smile and walk past the crowd of students agonizing about the exam and go treat yourself to something you enjoy. You just accomplished something notable. You took on the challenge of preparing well for a test, and regardless of the final grade, you need to get in the habit of praising yourself for your efforts.

A Word about Cheating—Don't!

Self-worth, of course, comes from knowing that you did the work honestly and did not cut any corners. Unfortunately, each year too many students attempt to get by through cheating. I could give you the high-minded explanation for why you should not cheat. Cheating is proof that you have not truly learned what you were taught and reflects a complete failure of time and tuition dollars. It's also an insult to yourself and anyone else paying for, or cheering on, your college education. If you are truly uninterested in putting in enough effort to learn, then why are you even attending college in the first place?

If, instead, you are having difficulty with the material and don't believe you can pass the class any other way, you really need high-powered intervention, which should be no shame at all. Chapter 6 offers strategies for what to do in this situation, none of which advise cutting corners. If you are having difficulty understanding the material in one class, you may well have similar problems in another class. Rather than seeking to "get by" through cheating, you are much better off trying to understand what the problem is and then working to remedy it. Maybe you have an undiagnosed learning disability. If so, that's unlikely to go away on its own. Cheating only allows you to run around—or more likely, run away from—the problem. What you need to do is treat it.

The Consequences

If none of these reasons convinces you to avoid cheating, let me offer a cold, hard reality check. Chances are you will be caught eventually, and the consequences can be severe. At some schools, most notably the University of Virginia, all students and faculty sign an honor code. Everyone must agree to standards of academic honesty, and they are also obliged to turn in others suspected of cheating. In fact, if a UVa student is aware of cheating and does not report the incident, she can be found guilty of violating the honor code. At schools like UVa, there are lots of eyes scouring the student body (and sometimes even the faculty) for cheating.

Even if your school is not this strict, it assuredly maintains an academic integrity policy that prohibits cheating or academic dishonesty. At one of my former schools, the policy covered not only cheating but also lying about academic work. If I were to suspect a student of cheating and asked him about it, he would be violating the college policy if he lied to me about his cheating. Violations of honor codes can be dealt with harshly. First-time cheaters are likely to earn an F on the test, if not fail the entire course, and repeat offenders may be kicked out of the university.

A violation also earns a mark on a student's transcript, telling all who read it that the student has been disciplined for dishonesty. Students invariably fail to appreciate the consequences of this notation, but in many ways it can be more serious than failing a class. Prospective employers often ask applicants to send along their college transcripts, and many an aspiring employee has been cut short by such a notation. A graduate who seeks a job with a government agency, particularly one that requires security clearance, is unlikely to pass the background investigation with a record of cheating. The same goes for applicants who seek jobs in fields offering access to confidential data or money. Would-be doctors or lawyers also may find themselves denied admission to professional schools for fear that they don't possess the ethics necessary to serve patients or clients. A mark of cheating means that you will always be in the position of having to explain why you did it and then convincingly argue why it's unlikely that you will do so again. Cheating may not be professional suicide, but it certainly seems like a severe self-inflicted wound.

I have no doubt that you know people who have cheated in high school. According to national studies, between 60 and 80 percent of American high school students have admitted cheating in school.[12] So it is likely that you, too, may have cheated on a test before you got to college. You may even have gotten away with it. But as ingenious as you or your classmates may have been in high school, know that we professors have already seen these tricks in college: students who copy off each other's exams, bring crib sheets and attempt to hide them in any number of places, imbed notes in electronic gadgetry, confer with or leave notes for one another in the bathroom during an exam, even use codes of synchronized coughing or tapping of pencils. There is very little that is new in cheating, although some students always seem to be pushing the envelope. Faculty are on the lookout for these techniques, and the very best professors structure exams to provide students the fewest opportunities to cheat. An open-book, open-notes essay exam, for example, offers little incentive for students to cheat, because there is nothing to memorize or spout back. You can't fake good thinking, which ultimately is what an effective exam seeks to measure.

You Don't Need to Cheat

I should add that I am sympathetic to some of the reasons students attempt to cheat. I understand that in an ever-competitive American economy, students may feel pressured to secure good grades to move on to graduate school or land the job of their dreams. Many students are accustomed to the thinking that says you should pursue every advantage to score your best. (How else do college admissions counselors or SAT tutors support themselves?) I am not saying that precollege coaching is the same as cheating—although I would ask whether these advantages are available to students regardless of their family's means—but I do recognize a connection between an attitude that says "do everything you can to be admitted" and students feeling pressured to cut corners to boost their grades.

Really, if you follow the other steps I have been recommending throughout this book, your grades will eventually take care of themselves. I cannot promise you straight As, but you should still earn solid marks. That alone should be enough to avoid cheating, but there is one last reason to swear off deceit—your own self-respect. Jump forward in your mind to graduation day. You're wearing your cap and gown, standing in the middle of your family, and people are snapping photos. Now, compare how you will feel if you know you have done honest, hard work versus cutting corners by cheating. Put aside for the moment the possibility that you may have a permanent mark on your transcript. I'm talking about how you will feel about yourself, whether you can truly look yourself in the mirror at the end of those four years and offer the person in the reflection genuine congratulations and respect. Your self-respect is too valuable to sell out by cheating, so make it easy on all of us by doing honest work.

5

WRITING PAPERS

It is sometimes said that writers feel a compulsion to write each day. I know of one author, in fact, who insists on writing two hours a day, no matter what. If he has been away from his office all day and then goes out for the evening, he still returns to his computer for two hours of writing before bed.

For the rest of us, writing may seem like a chore at times, especially when the assignment is not one of our choosing. But papers are a fact of college life, so you might as well develop a strategy for knocking them out effectively. Papers are required in a wide variety of college classes, from the traditional introductory English course to upper-level classes in your major. Papers also come in a variety of shapes and sizes. Many are likely to be in the three-to-five-page variety, in which the instructor asks you to analyze readings assigned in the class. But you also may see assignments as short as one page, in which you are asked to provide a brief reaction to class discussion, or as long as twenty pages, which is often the standard length for a research term paper.

Regardless of the type or length of the paper, your instructor is essentially asking you to do the same thing: to analyze and answer a question by applying previous writings, empirical data, or your own research to reach a conclusion that you can justify. Of course, that only gets you to the starting point of writing, because in a paper it is not enough simply to have good ideas; you also have to be able to convey them clearly. Think of a paper, then, as having three parts: first, you need to conduct your research, a stage that will undoubtedly vary with the length and type of the assignment; second, you must organize your thoughts into a logical order with which to answer the question assigned; finally, you need to write, a process that itself is also divided into three parts—the initial draft, the revision, and final editing.

I'll take you through each of those various stages, explaining how you should address them based on the kind of paper assigned. I also offer some benchmarks to help you plan your time. It doesn't matter how quickly you turned out your high school papers; college papers are different. They are usually longer and more involved, and are assigned in most of your classes throughout the term. Despite that popular image of the college all-nighter, there really is no substitute for adequate preparation and comprehensive editing in crafting an excellent paper.

Believe it or not, your professors really want you to succeed at paper writing. Generally, we would be delighted if the entire class wrote "A" papers. It's not that we're trying to avoid the prospect of wading through a pile of mediocre papers, having to chug coffee just to keep ourselves engaged. We admire good arguments and fine writing—and we want to see those from you. If you fail to retain anything else from this chapter, then just remember this one point: if you are prepared to do your part by starting your paper early and devoting sufficient time to the research, writing, and editing, your professor or other writing instructors will be there to help. Whether through office hours, e-mailed comments, or individual tutoring from your school's writing center, it is possible to write—and be appropriately rewarded for—a good paper. I cannot promise you a Pulitzer Prize for your work, but this is truly a situation in which your level of effort can significantly affect the result.

Planning

No matter how short the paper, you need to leave yourself sufficient time to do the reading and research, put together an outline, create a first draft, and revise and edit your work. By sufficient time, I mean much longer than one night, even as I watch students turn in term papers that they started just a few days (or even a few hours) before they were due. It will take a little practice, but you need to get a feel for the speed at which you can make your way through these various processes. How many pages per hour can you write when working on a first draft? If it helps, I'm still stuck at two to three double-spaced pages per hour, even using the fastest word processing software. (Don't get me started telling you what it was like in the "olden days" before computers.) But my composing speed does not account for the much greater time that I must spend researching and finding the sources from which to make my arguments, the time I set aside for outlining my thoughts, or the hours it takes me to revise and edit that initial draft. For a five-page paper, I may spend as many as fifteen hours from start to finish, and I do this professionally. Come to think of it, you do too, so let's work through a reasonable plan for your papers.

Making a Calendar

A lot of the planning process rests on the type of paper you're being asked to complete. Does the professor expect you to conduct research outside of class, or are you limited to the sources you have already covered in the classroom? How large a bibliography are you supposed to produce? This will drive the amount of research you must do. And of course, how many pages is the assignment? You should start your planning process by working backward from the due date. Let's imagine you have a sixteen-page research paper due in your English class on November 17. This is a substantial assignment, so the first thing you should do is highlight November 16 in your calendar as the assumed due date. If at all possible, you should give yourself an extra day's grace period in your planning to permit a final read-through and account for any unexpected delays that may arise in your research and writing. Next, estimate the number of hours that you will need to write the first draft and the number of hours you will have available to work on the paper. If you can write at a rate of two pages an hour, you would need eight hours to produce the first draft of the paper (16 pages × 2 pages per hour = 8 hours of writing). If you usually spend two hours per day working on your English projects, then it would take four days to write this first draft.

Now, set aside about half that time to revise the paper. Not edit—revise. Even if your first drafts are good, you'll undoubtedly find arguments that don't flow together, sections that need more support, and lines that call for better construction. Make sure you leave a day between the initial draft and the revisions just to clear your head. Then wait at least another day and start the editing process. For this, you'll need about half the time of your revisions, but you'll still want to take the opportunity to read the paper through for grammar, style, and spelling. At this point, we've already figured on almost ten days of preparation: four days for writing, a day to put the document aside, two days for revisions, another day to put the document aside, one day to edit the paper, and a final day as insurance against unforeseen circumstances. So for a paper due on November 17, you need to start the writing process by November 7.

Of course, we haven't yet figured in the time you will need to conduct your research and craft your outline and arguments. Research usually takes—or, I should say, ought to take—at least as long as the writing and editing of the first draft, and organizing the sources you have identified and crafting a workable outline may be about a quarter of that time. Lest this sound like an exaggeration, know that it takes considerable skill to understand the significance of the findings you have uncovered and construct an argument that logically flows from point to point with sufficient support from your research.

So looking at the calendar again, if it took you eight hours to write the first draft and two more hours to edit it after the revisions, then you're looking at those same ten hours of research and up to two additional hours to organize your sources and construct an outline. Figuring that you plan on working two hours per day on your paper, we're talking another six days of preparation. All told, then, you would expect to work a total of twenty-six hours on this term paper—ten for research, two to organize your sources and craft an outline, eight to write a first draft, four to revise it, and two to edit. Figuring a few days to put the drafting aside in the middle, you ought to begin work November 1 for a paper due November 17.

Calendar for a major paper

Sunday	Monday	Tuesday	Wednesday	Thursday	Friday	Saturday
1 Research	2 Research	3 Research	4 Research	5 Research	6 Organization and outline	7 Writing
8 Writing	9 Writing	10 Writing	11 Open day	12 Revisions	13 Revisions	14 Open day
15 Editing	16 Due date for yourself	17 **Paper Due**				

Note that in the schedule, I'm not distinguishing between weekdays or weekends, nor am I figuring on personal travel during the middle of the paper. Most term papers are due at the end of the semester, which in the fall comes not too long after Thanksgiving break. Too often, students figure they will bring the paper along on their visit home, only to find themselves returning to school five days later having done nothing, because they understandably wanted to hang out with family and friends. So if you take that time off while the paper is pending, plan on extra days for the work.

For that matter, you may want to add an extra day or two in the middle of the paper to seek feedback from your instructor. Depending on the individual, professors are often willing to review interim drafts of class papers. Generally, the more substantial the paper assigned, the more open your professors will be to talking over paper ideas, examining outlines, and sometimes reading first drafts. The same formula should apply to your overtures. The higher the stakes for the paper, the more effort you should make to see if your outline meets the instructor's expectations or your draft makes sense. For additional help with your papers, most schools maintain writing-skills centers where you can get extra instruction, feedback, or editing. These resources are discussed at greater length in chapter 6. For now, make a note that you may want to set aside time in the schedule for your paper to seek outside help.

The calendar sketched above is a model approach to a term paper. Clearly, if your paper assignment is for fewer pages or does not require much outside research, you can shorten the time you dedicate to the project. For that matter, you can choose to work more than two hours per day on the assignment, thus reducing the number of days you must dedicate to the project. But let's also be realistic and acknowledge that what I have proposed is the ideal. I am under no illusion that most students will spend this much time on a paper—even a term paper that can be worth more than a quarter of a course grade. I would not be surprised to see students reduce the amount of time they dedicate to their papers to one-half of what I have outlined.

But remember that this book is designed to help get you through college with the greatest chance at success, both in the education you are receiving and the grades you are earning. If you want to produce your best work, then you really need to put in the time on the project. Leaving things until the last minute or seeking to compose an entire twenty-page paper in one (very long) night is almost always a recipe for disaster. If you do nothing else, take the time when the paper is first assigned to block out your work schedule for the project. Then reward yourself along the way for meeting those markers. If you have set aside four hours to research a short paper and you accomplish the work one evening, then stop and do something that makes you happy: see a movie, hang out with friends, go out for a meal, anything to get yourself in the habit of sticking with the schedule you have set for yourself. As a friend of mine likes to say, these are "life skills," the kind of work habits you will need once you graduate from college and make that first foray into a career. So not only will you give yourself the best shot at a good grade on your papers, you also will build the kind of skills and habits that will reward you in the professional world.

Conducting the Research

My children went to public elementary school in Virginia. In the Old Dominion, fourth-grade students spend the year learning about Virginia history, so much so that my son used to joke that the motto for his class was "all Virginia all of the time." Imagine my surprise, then, when I learned that my children's social studies textbook included language declaring that thousands of African American soldiers fought *for* the South during the Civil War. This is a pretty provocative claim—that slaves would have fought willingly for their captors. It is also wrong. Who could have included such erroneous material in an elementary school textbook assigned throughout the state? The answer, I quickly came to learn, was a textbook author "who is not a trained historian and who said she found the information about black Confederate soldiers on the Internet."[1] Apparently, the author came across claims by the group Sons of Confederate Veterans that slaves willingly fought for the South and decided to include these claims as fact in her textbook, *Our Virginia: Past and Present*. Sons of Confederate Veterans, by the way, is the same group that also "disputes the widely accepted conclusion that the struggle over slavery was the main cause of the Civil War."[2]

For those of us who make our living at scholarship and who are required to support any claims we make—whether as fact or opinion—with sufficient proof, the Virginia textbook fiasco was an abomination. As historians quickly pointed out, the research is nearly "unanimous in calling [the] accounts of black Confederate soldiers a misrepresentation of history."[3] In response, officials from Virginia's Department of Education had to take to the airwaves, conceding awkwardly that "just because a book is approved doesn't mean [the state] endorses every sentence" in it.[4] The textbook has since been corrected.

Virginia's mistake should be your lesson in carefully considering the source of any research you employ in your papers. Just because a source exists does not necessarily make it credible. Walk through a grocery store's checkout aisle at some point and glance at the headlines of the weekly tabloids. Do you really believe that an alien fathered the latest movie's star's child? I certainly hope not. But do you apply the same skepticism to the postings you read on the Web? In these days in which anyone with access to a laptop can start an urban legend, it is all the more important to carefully verify what you read.

Credibility versus Truth

In academe, we address the question of verification by requiring authors to navigate a peer-review process before their work is published in a journal or book. That is, researchers submit their papers or manuscripts to a potential publisher, who shares the work anonymously with up to three experts in the particular field who then read and comment on the quality of the research and writing. Was the research done correctly? Are the findings credible? Did the authors correctly attribute prior research? These are only some of the questions that the reviewers are asked to consider. In addition to improving the quality of any works accepted for publication, the double-blind peer-review[5] process is intended to weed out research that is suspect and unreliable.

It's important not to confuse reliability with absolute truth when considering peer-reviewed academic research. Scholars can differ with one another on the same subject, and, in fact, research findings may contradict one another even when scholars have conducted credible research. Consider regular debates over Americans' voting behavior. One set of scholars may conduct a poll of voters and conclude that the public is motivated by disdain for incumbents. Other researchers may look at the same poll and claim that voters' economic fears are the true source of the motivation. Some journals may even publish dueling articles from these authors as a kind of point-counterpoint for readers to consider. That the two sets of authors disagree with each other does not mean you should dismiss either or both of the articles. Rather, in surviving the peer-review process at an academic journal, both positions are plausible. The reader is then left to consider which view makes more sense.

Sources

Your goal in conducting research for a paper, then, is twofold. First you have to decide which sources are reliable to use, then you must weigh the merits of the conclusions or arguments presented. You will rarely go wrong in relying on scholarly sources—books from academic presses and articles published in peer-reviewed journals. By academic presses, I mean publishers sponsored by universities. The publisher of this book, for example, the University of Chicago Press, is one of the most respected in the world because its editors carefully seek out top scholarship and employ tough peer-review standards in selecting works. But there are other fine nonacademic presses that regularly publish high-quality scholarship—for example, Routledge or Congressional Quarterly.

Questionable Material

The books you need to question are those that are not based on research, per se, but instead reflect an author's "take" on an issue. Here, I'm thinking of books like Bill O'Reilly's *Pinheads and Patriots: Where You Stand in the Age of Obama* or Al Franken's *Rush Limbaugh is a Big Fat Idiot*. Neither could ever be said to advance scholarship, and despite their protestations on air, in their heart of hearts both authors assuredly know there is nothing objective about their books. Still, you *can* employ books like these in your research, so long as you recognize *how* and *for what purposes* you can cite them. No reasonable scholar—and by that I mean your professor—would ever accept political polemics like O'Reilly's or Franken's as "proof" of the points that each author raises. For example, Franken's claim that the "No Child Left Behind [law was] the most ironically named piece of legislation since the 1942 Japanese Family Leave" would hardly be acceptable support for that conclusion in a paper about education reform.[6] His is clearly a biting and sarcastic take on conservative politics in America, and he intentionally does not offer research to support his point, because the purpose is to inflame and entertain. The same is true for most of the caustic titles you see in airport bookstores from authors like Ann Coulter, Glenn Beck, or Keith

Olbermann. These books are most certainly not scholarly sources and should not be introduced in a paper as proof of the opinions voiced. But you *can* use books like these as evidence of the authors' beliefs. If, for example, you are arguing that President Obama's policies inflamed conservatives, then books by O'Reilly and Beck provide good support for your point. Here, you're not claiming the commentators' opinions are necessarily true; rather, the fact that they have these views is supportive of your larger point.

Safe Sources

This distinction between sources as proof of the arguments raised in them and sources as evidence that a particular fact occurred is central to determining which references you can reliably use in a college paper. If your point is that a particular event occurred—a meeting was held, an election took place, a study was released—then you are generally safe using many types of sources. What you are looking for are publications in which an editor or someone other than the author has fact-checked the account. Sources like these typically include newspapers, magazines, or books. If, instead, you are making a claim about the state of knowledge at a given time—for example, whether cigarettes cause cancer—you ought to rely on scholarly sources from those disciplines that are reporting peer-reviewed research. You might still be able to make this point from news accounts, for example, by using a story from your local paper summarizing the views of medical experts, but you are running the risk that the reporters may not understand the science involved or that they have skewed accounts by focusing only on those sources who were easiest to reach.

Borderline Sources

The gray zone is when you are seeking to make an argument about social phenomena using mixed sources. Let's say, for example, that you are writing a paper on lobbying groups and that you are tasked with assessing the effectiveness of the American Association of Retired Persons. Presumably, you would draw from academic research discussing the typical tactics and activities of lobbying groups and additional scholarly literature about how lobbying is carried out. But you might want to include accounts from actors in the political process about their interactions with the AARP and whether they consider the organization to have been especially effective. Or you might pull from a journalistic case study of the lobbying surrounding a particular piece of legislation to evaluate the effectiveness of the AARP.

In each of these situations, you would want to investigate stories in a variety of news periodicals—daily newspapers, magazines, or Washington weeklies, and you might also investigate newsletters from the AARP or others lobbying groups for accounts of what the AARP did and how others reacted. The key in these situations is understanding your purpose in citing a particular source. The news stories, for example, will likely tell you what the AARP did, and they may even help to answer why the organization undertook a particular action. But those stories alone cannot establish whether the AARP's activities were effective. To reach that conclusion you must draw on the accounts of what happened and then analyze those reports against the scholarly literature on activist groups. Similarly, an organization's claim of legislative success in its newsletter cannot be accepted at face value but instead must be compared against other reports you uncover about the details and results of the larger legislative campaign.

The Dreaded Wikipedia

Any discussion of credible sources must address the Internet. If you are like most college students (or faculty, for that matter), you are likely on the Web for a good portion of the day. If you need directions, you go to MapQuest; if you need information, you use Google; and if you have a question, you look at Wikipedia. I'm no different. But whereas all of these sites are a good starting place for information, none of them should be seen as a reliable source for an academic paper. This is most acute in the case of Wikipedia, which has become the siren song for many college students and the bane of most professors' existence. Believe me, I get Wikipedia's allure. The site is easy to find, it covers a lot of ground, and it looks scholarly. I even admire its overall objective of generating shared and evolving explanations for encyclopedic facts. But Wikipedia simply cannot be relied upon for academic research, as there is no way of assessing the credibility of its source material.

Suppose I decided to post to a Wikipedia entry on allergies. I've had allergies most of my life and feel pretty comfortable explaining how they feel. Plus, I'm armed with just enough knowledge to be able to speak generally about the sources of allergies. But really, do you want to rely on me—a social scientist and lawyer—to explain the causes of allergies and recommend a treatment, or would you feel more comfortable hearing from a real allergist? The same thing could be true for aviation. I have about fifteen hours of flying toward my private pilot's license and am a regular connoisseur of aviation magazines. But if you're trying to understand why a thousand-pound aluminum tube is able to defy gravity, wouldn't you be better off hearing the explanation from a commercial pilot? Until Wikipedia identifies its posters and provides readers an opportunity to evaluate their qualifications, its entries cannot be considered entirely reliable. Even if we presume that inaccurate posts will be corrected eventually, those corrections are decided upon collectively by Wikipedia's readers, about whom we know next to nothing. So do yourselves and your instructors a favor and resist the temptation to cite Wikipedia in your papers. You will be saving us all a lot of red ink.

Other Web Postings

If Wikipedia is a problematic source, you can only imagine what I am going to say about other websites. Actually, that message is no different from what I've advised about old-line media: you need to be a critical consumer of information. In this age when anyone can post to the Web, where the slightest urge leads to an immediate Twitter update, you have to sift through what you find online to determine which sources are credible and for what purposes. Just because someone said it online doesn't necessarily make it true. Perhaps this should be the title of a modern country song, but for your purposes, the mantra should be stenciled above your computer. Check who has posted the information; ask about their qualifications, their basis to know the information, and their potential biases. Consider whether their postings establish a fact or are merely proof of an opinion. Ask whether anyone has tested or fact checked their post. Then (and only then) will you be in a position to decide how to use the information.

How to Find Sources

These are not simply the complaints of an academic relic who wants you to go to the library and read a book. Although I would love to hear that you know where your campus library is and that you have actually been inside and cracked open a book, I am much more concerned that you use reliable information. This *can* be done online, and in fact, I am a big proponent of electronic research. At most universities now, a panoply of scholarly journals is available online. You can search for a term, identify a set of articles that addresses this topic, and browse and download the full texts of relevant articles, all with the click of a mouse. Electronic research has saved both students and faculty alike countless hours in the library.

At the risk of proving once more that I attended college in the dark ages, up through the 1990s, almost all academic research was done in hard-copy format. Students would consult a digest or index of terms that would point them to various journals or articles that covered the topic. Then students would fan out to the library stacks, scrunched into small corridors pouring over compilations of academic journals in poor fluorescent light. Today we can conduct the same research in a fraction of the time from our laptops. That is progress.

But just as electronic access has eased the burden of academic research, it has raised scholars' responsibilities to evaluate the credibility of online sources. Stick with peer-reviewed journals and you're fine. But if you choose to consider other sources—which you should—make sure you can establish a source's credibility and understand for what purposes you can use it. If you don't ask yourself those questions as you're preparing your paper, your professor most certainly will when grading it.

The Four Steps of Research

Ultimately, I recommend a four-step process for conducting research: online searches to narrow the field, an examination of scholarly articles and books, a review of popular media, and a search of available databases. The longer and more involved the paper, the greater and more in depth the research process must be. This should be made clear in the instructions for the assignment. Does the professor explain whether you are supposed to do research and, if so, whether you are expected to go beyond the readings in the class? There are some assignments in which you will be expected simply to comment on the reading you have already done. I often assign short papers like these to graduate students. Typically, the class will read a book or a series of articles for our weekly meetings, and in the week beforehand I will assign them a question about those readings to answer in a two-to-three-page memo.

On an assignment like this, I do not expect (and frankly do not want to burden students with) additional research.

Online Searches

If, however, the assignment says you need to conduct outside research, it's time to implement the four-step process. First, you should conduct some online searches with Google or another search engine just to get a flavor of the arguments offered about the subject and a sense of what some of the likely sources may be. For example, if the paper asks you to analyze the allusions in Herman Melville's *Moby Dick*, a Google search might present you with a nearly fifty-year-old article that appeared in *Modern Language Quarterly*.[7] You might also come across a posting at the website 123helpme.com that offers several examples of allusions in the book.[8] Neither of these sources should be seen as dispositive, and, in the case of the latter, the entry offers neither the author's identity nor other information to assess the credibility of the sources. Rather, they are a starting point to inform you of the range of material out there for consideration and a road map to other sources you might want to consult. Of course, if you do end up using any of the sources you find on your initial Internet search, make sure that you cite them.

Scholarly Articles and Books

Your next stop, and the place where you should spend most of your time researching, is academic journals. These come with such titles as the *American Political Science Review*, the *Annals of Human Biology*, or even the *Journal of the History of Sexuality*. The easiest way to locate these journals is to talk to your college's reference librarian about how to access the electronic research databases that most schools maintain for faculty and students. These tools are fantastic, allowing you to search by topic area, article title, or author's name, among other possibilities. The trick, of course, is using a search term sufficiently broad to return sources on your paper while narrow enough that you're not retrieving hundreds of possible articles that are off topic.

Broadly speaking, so long as you are searching in one of the research databases provided by your school's library, you will be picking up articles in peer-reviewed journals. There are some exceptions, however. Law reviews are actually edited by law students, not professors or lawyers, but the work that appears in law journals is generally sufficiently scholarly that you can use it in a paper. You may also come across professional newsletters. For example, *Anthropology in Action* is listed online as a newsletter. This means that the publication is a vehicle for scholars and practitioners in the field to share news or announcements about professional happenings and in some cases to publish shorter synopses of research findings. You should tread carefully with newsletters, as the level of research that appears in them is not as sophisticated as it is in a peer-reviewed journal and, in fact, oftentimes is not peer reviewed at all. If you have a question about the suitability of a source, you should consult your professor before you use it in your paper.

In addition to academic journals, you should consult scholarly books. You remember those things, right? Bulky, bound hard copies found in libraries. Or, perhaps you have a Kindle or iPad and read your books electronically. In either event, books are a tremendous resource for student papers. Because they are longer than articles, books often can cover an entire field and provide an excellent overview of a subject. They also can be found in the same manner as articles, since college library catalogs can typically be searched electronically. To expedite your research, consult the index of a book first to figure out which pages of text will be most pertinent to your paper.

Popular Media

Next, you may wish to consider newspapers or news magazines. News stories can provide you contemporaneous accounts of facts of events. For example, if you were writing a paper on changed attitudes in America as a result of the September 11 terrorist attacks, you might want to explain what happened and how people felt in the days immediately following the hijackings. By consulting the archives of the *New York Times* or other respected national newspapers, you would undoubtedly find stories describing the attitudes of people near Ground Zero in New York as well as Americans farther away but no less touched by the attacks. Most major newspapers and magazines can be searched using the online tool LexisNexis, which your school probably has.

Databases

Finally, you should consider publicly available databases, such as demographic data provided by the U.S. Bureau of the Census or archived datasets maintained by the Inter-University Consortium for Political and Social Research. The ICPSR, as it is known, is an "international consortium of about 700 academic institutions and research organizations [that] maintains a data archive of more than 500,000 files of research in the social sciences." Among other things, it "hosts 16 specialized collections of data in education, aging, criminal justice, substance abuse, terrorism, and other fields."[9]

Each of the electronic sources I have mentioned should be available through your college's library. If for some reason your school does not have access, you might consider a trip to a larger institution's library for your research. Many schools offer entry to visiting researchers and will make their online databases available to you while you conduct the research for your paper. Electronic research is so much more convenient than the former hard-copy method that you really should go out of your way to gain electronic access. In a few instances, however, you will have to rely on old-fashioned hard copies. If, for example, your research involves original historical texts, you likely will have to sequester yourself in an archive to review documents by hand. But this will be the case for only the most advanced undergraduate theses.

Compiling and Organizing the Research

As you read through articles or other material, it is important to take notes from the documents. Before computers, students used index cards for their research, creating a separate card for each important point presented in the reading. Nowadays, we all use computers for note taking, but the practice is no less important. As you read through a document, write up a summary of the relevant points that could be useful for your paper. When you come across essential quotations, type these up too. If you can, it's fine to cut and paste parts of the document you're reading into your own notes, but only if you take great care to use quotation marks and cite any material that comes from someone else.

You should be doing this in your own notes as well so that you do not become confused about which parts of your notes are derived from other sources. This is a particular hazard if you cut and paste from the articles you read, since a pasted passage can easily blend in with your own notes. Over the years I have seen more than a dozen students laid low by a plagiarism charge because they forgot to make a note of material they had copied from another source and thus accidentally included a passage in their final papers without attribution. Whether intentional or not, even these accidents count as plagiarism, and, as I discuss later in this chapter, plagiarism is the academic equivalent of a capital offense. One way to avoid this predicament is to use a reference or note-taking program as you review new sources and type them into your notes. Software programs like EndNote, Biblioscape, and Ref-Works provide an electronic template for note taking and store your references for uniform citation in the final paper.

When to Stop

It's difficult to say when you have conducted enough research. Often, it's simply a matter of running out of time. If you need to start drafting the paper five days before it is due and that deadline has come, then you'll need to bring your research to a close. But if you're not racing the clock, there are three general rules that signal when it's time to close the research. First, does the assignment list a number of sources you must employ for the paper, and have you consulted that many? If your professor insists on at least eight sources and you're only at six, then you know you still have more to go. On the other hand, if you already have consulted twelve sources, you have looked at enough.

Second, do you feel that you have answered your own questions about the topic, and do you believe you can create a coherent argument? No matter the number of sources, if you don't feel you have enough information on which to craft a solid argument, then you need to keep researching. However, if you have been through ten or more sources and still feel confused, then you ought to make an appointment with your professor to talk about your research strategy. Perhaps you have been chasing down a dead-end path and your instructor can help direct you to more fruitful sources. Faculty are unlikely to be sympathetic to student requests if you haven't immersed yourself in the literature beforehand. But if you have been at the research awhile and still feel adrift, your professor is an obvious, and likely welcoming, resource.

Finally, if additional sources continue to cite to the same seminal articles or books, then you know you have done a good job of uncovering the central texts or arguments. Although further research may provide a more nuanced take on the subject, you should feel confident that you already have an essential understanding of the topic.

Organizing Your Notes

In some ways, research is the easy part of writing a paper. The more difficult stages are organizing the material you have uncovered into useable chunks and then structuring them into common themes or points. There is no magic formula or secret shortcut for this. As you read back over your notes, a good starting point is to craft distinct headings for what you have uncovered and then move your notes around so that the various points referenced fall under them. Let's say, for example, that you are writing a paper on childhood obesity and several of the articles you have read include statistics on the number of American children who are obese. You might create a heading titled "Obesity Statistics" and then move all of the statistics you have found to that one section. This is a delicate responsibility, as you must remember to attach the appropriate citations to each statistic, quotation, or section that you move. But once you get the hang of this, it's not too difficult.

To continue this hypothetical, let's say that the articles also have statistical information on childhood obesity in other countries. This would be another heading—"Comparative Obesity Statistics"—where you would move the data you had uncovered on different countries' obesity rates. The idea here is to create sufficient headings so that all of the information you have uncovered can be either categorized or discarded. Once you have those categories, you can move the concepts around on the page until you have a logical flow to the story or argument you are making.

Returning to the paper on childhood obesity, the two categories of statistics suggest a natural contrast between America and other nations. What might the reasons be for these differences, and what do the categories in the rest of your notes have to say about these divergent realities? This is how you begin to build an outline for your paper. It's almost like completing a jigsaw puzzle, as you think through the ways that the various categories of research fit together. Once you have a structure that makes sense to you, it's time to incorporate the various citations back into the categories so that you have an annotated structure for the research you have completed.

The Parts of a Paper

Note that this is not yet an outline; rather, it's a way of organizing your research so that you understand what it says and how the various points or findings you have uncovered fit together. The next stage is to step back and put together your arguments. How you approach this depends on the kind of paper you have been assigned. A five-page English paper asking you to compare an author's use of metaphor calls for fewer arguments than a twenty-five-page physics paper in which you are supposed to evaluate the theory of relativity. Still most papers require five distinct sections: 1) an introduction in which you describe the issue you are covering, present your ultimate take, and explain its significance; 2) a literature review or background section in writing in which you describe and evaluate prior writings or research on the subject; 3) an analysis section in which you explain your ultimate conclusion on the question assigned; 4) a discussion section in which you describe the significance or the ramifications of the findings you have reached; and 5) a closing section in which you link your conclusions to prior work on the subject and restate the significance of your answer to the question asked.

Obviously, the shorter the assigned paper, the shorter these sections will be. In a two-page paper, for example, you would hardly devote much space to a literature review, other than to provide some background on the issues being analyzed. By the same token, in an undergraduate thesis—especially one involving the social or natural sciences—your analysis section would likely be lengthy and would describe the methods and tests you undertook and as well as the results you uncovered and whether they are reliable.

The Introduction

Regardless of which type of paper you are writing or how long its length, it is crucial to begin your paper with a strong opening paragraph or section. The introduction needs to do three things—grab the reader's attention, describe the question to be examined and its significance, and provide a road map for the reader to follow the rest of the paper. Feel free to be creative in that first paragraph, using a vivid example that helps to introduce the topic, but be careful that you don't get so carried away that your overture becomes an unnecessary tangent. Most importantly, you should explain to the reader what your argument will be and how to anticipate its presentation. Not only does this kind of structure help the reader to follow your logic throughout the paper, it also is a quick tip-off to your instructor of a well-organized assignment. Students who don't leave enough time for preparation and thus find themselves composing at the keyboard are almost never able to provide this kind of introductory outline because, too often, they begin typing before they know exactly where they are headed.

The Analysis

The most important parts of your paper are the analysis and discussion sections. Your task is to convince the reader of the merits of your thesis or argument, a job that requires you to engage existing data, research, or past writings and explain how the evidence you introduce supports the overall conclusion you reach. All too often, students see these sections as an opportunity simply to recount their opinion of a subject. Even if the opinion is a reasonable one, stating one's views without explaining where they come from and why they are credible is hardly convincing. Indeed, I know many professors who tell their students some version of the admonition, "I don't care what you believe; I care what you think and whether you can prove it." That skill—the ability to explain and support one's positions—is perhaps the single greatest distinction between competent college graduates and untrained incoming students. All of us have our own beliefs, a fact that is borne out every day in the thousands of blog postings on subjects far and wide. But the mark of an educated thinker is the ability to persuade others of her views by reason. That is no truer than in your college papers.

To help my students in mastering this skill, I sometimes suggest they follow the acronym **PEAR**. First, state your **p**osition or conclusion. Then **e**xplain it. Consider **a**lternative views that might disagree with yours. Then close by **r**esponding to those possible objections, showing why your original position is still a reasonable conclusion. Although the exercise may feel a little artificial at first, it is a virtually foolproof method to ensure that you have truly explained your conclusions and haven't simply stated your opinions without justification. Besides being a useful tool for crafting a paper, PEAR is also an effective rule to guide you through college in general. No one is expecting that you must change your opinions from the start of a course until its end, but if you don't consider alternative points and stand ready to refute disagreeable ones with effective arguments, then neither of us has really done our job.

In the end, you will change some of your views in college—and, indeed, you should as you encounter new approaches, data, and arguments that are convincing. To some extent, that is the point of a paper—to get you thinking deeply about an issue of concern and to conduct to answer it. The exercise requires that you teach yourself so that the findings or conclusions you reach come from your own deeper thinking and analysis and not because a professor seemed to lecture in favor of them in class. This is why it's so important to explain your conclusions—so your professor can follow and appreciate the thinking that has gone into your paper. Believe me, we read *plenty* of papers over the course of an academic year. When we come across a paper with solid conclusions and well-reasoned explanations, we are almost as tickled as you in your achievement.

Writing Style

If the best papers are a treat, it is only because they are not commonplace. Talk to any professor outside of the English department, and you will hear similar complaints about students' approach to writing: why is it that students so often ask whether writing ability will count as part of the paper grade? (In fact, you may hear the same lament from your English teachers as well.) On some level, I understand this question. If a class is not a composition course, then presumably the professor is more interested in the substance of students' ideas than their writing ability. But ultimately, any class is trying to teach students how to communicate their ideas effectively. At a most basic level, then, the ability to write is a prerequisite for an effective essay.

Notice that I said "the ability to write," not necessarily "the ability to write *well*." Although faculty members undoubtedly wish that all of their students could write well, we do not require excellent writing ability in non-composition courses. The writing ability I mention is the more basic skill of constructing a sensible sentence or paragraph. I am continually shocked by how many students miss such grammatical constructions as subject-verb agreement or who use apostrophes to denote a plural noun rather than simply adding an "s" to the word. These are things they should have learned in high school.

Write a Poor First Draft

But there is no point in yammering away about problems that develop before students get to college. Once you and your friends arrive at college, your problems become my problems and those of my colleagues. So what are we asking of you in the writing of your papers?

First, we want you to take the time to do your best work. Ironically, this means allowing yourself the freedom to write a poor first draft. Yes, you heard me correctly. Remove as much pressure as you can from that first draft by vowing simply to get down your most basic ideas. If it helps, repeat this mantra to yourself throughout the first draft: "write crap."

Of course, neither of us wants an awful final version of your paper, but by giving yourself the latitude to write sloppily at first, to get half of your ideas down while mucking up the rest, you will keep writer's block at bay. And believe me, writer's block is torment. You sit motionless in front of your computer staring at the blinking cursor hoping that inspiration will arise at any moment. Yet, the longer you wait, the more nervous and frustrated you become that you aren't writing; even when you begin typing you may find yourself silently criticizing the work that appears on the screen.

Often the root cause for writer's block is fear—fear that you don't know what you're saying or that your work will be found wanting by readers. That's why the license of a poor rough draft can be liberating. Rather than waiting for inspiration, you just start writing; instead of criticizing yourself for what you have not yet perfected, you give yourself a base from which to revise and edit later. You will likely feel the momentum build as you see the cursor jump from one page to the next. Perhaps your writing will even get a little better as you move further into the first draft and develop a sense of flow. But even if you are not pleased with the content or style of what you're writing, keep repeating the mantra of the first draft, allowing yourself the latitude to write poorly at first. At initial draft can be improved; a blank page, by contrast, leaves you with nothing.

Revising and Editing

Of course, writing like this works only if you leave yourself sufficient time for serious revision and editing. As Justice Louis Brandeis is reported to have said, "There is no such thing as good writing, only good rewriting."[10] Thanks to technology, first drafts have gotten better since Justice Brandeis's time; with the advent of the computer and its backspace and delete buttons, it's nearly impossible for some writers to resist the urge to stop and correct errors as they construct their first copy. But even so, revising and editing are crucial steps that will improve and polish your paper. You cannot expect to sit down at your computer on a Sunday night with a deadline looming the next morning and crank out a decent five-page paper overnight. Besides the obvious issue of exhaustion, you'll be missing the opportunity to put your writing aside to return fresh for revisions and editing. Lest you think your instructors do not notice the difference, let me assure you that we do and that it matters.

Revising and Editing are Complementary

I mentioned both revising and editing your first draft because they are different processes. In revising your first draft, you are looking for changes needed in content or structure. Perhaps you'll notice that material in a later section of the draft really belongs in the background section, or you'll realize that two arguments should be flipped in order to make more sense. Sometimes you'll even conclude that you need to scrap whole sections and rewrite them completely. In revising your first draft you're trying to improve the substance of your paper and the logical flow of your arguments.

Once you are satisfied with the paper's structure, it's time to step back and edit your latest draft. This is when you closely scrutinize your writing for grammatical or spelling errors, word choice, and awkward expressions that could be presented more clearly. In editing your paper you are taking a good substantive piece and improving the mode of its presentation.

These two skills—revising and editing—really go hand-in-glove. Until you revise the substance and structure of your draft so that you are satisfied with both, there is no point in spending time or attention scrutinizing the writing. And by the time that you get to reading the paper through for grammar and word choice, it will be deflating to conclude that the structure still needs work. This is not to say that revising and editing always go in the same order, for there is nothing wrong (and, indeed, plenty to be gained) in catching grammatical errors while revising the structure of your draft. For that matter, if you're still unhappy with the substance of your argument by the time you get to the editing phase, it is better to stop then and improve the main points of your paper rather than polishing the writing style of an argument that leaves you dissatisfied. This is one of the many reasons that you need to leave sufficient time in your writing schedule for revisions and editing.

Good editing sometimes requires a second set of eyes, for example, a willing friend or relative to look over your writing and help you catch misspellings or awkward phrasing. But be careful that they only help you spot the errors, not write out the corrections for you. Ultimately, that paper needs to be your own work. If you prefer, you might ask them to read your paper out loud to you so that you can hear if your language sounds stilted or awkward. Stop them whenever you come to a problematic spot and ask them to note the phrase in the text so that you can go back to it later for corrections.

Spell Check Is Necessary

At a minimum, you must, must, must use spell check. There really is no excuse for avoiding it, as the program takes just minutes. Spell check is remarkably good at identifying potential misspellings. The tool still requires you to choose between possible options, but it is a godsend for the poor spellers among us. Failure to use spell check is tantamount to telling your professor, "I really didn't care about this paper enough to spend even five minutes checking for my misspellings." Laugh if you will, but I have seen plenty of papers in which students did not run spell check. They should be embarrassed.

Editing for Grammar

If I'm a fan of spell check, I unfortunately cannot recommend grammar check. I've seen it make too many errors, especially when writers want to use a more advanced construction. This does not mean, however, that you can take grammatical errors off your check list. Depending upon your professor, you may be expected to know only such basic skills as proper punctuation and capitalization, whereas in other classes your writing may be held to more advanced rules like compound modifiers. Frankly, each professor has his or her pet peeves in writing, although not all of us share those with students. Rather than list all of those grammatical errors here, you should take the time to consult a grammar book, or even better, review a website hosted by a college writing program that not only lists common grammatical errors but also presents useful examples to help you prevent these mistakes in your own work.[11]

I can hear you now—"He wants me to what?! I already know how to write or I wouldn't have been admitted to college in the first place. I don't need to be bothered with reading a boring grammar book or website, because my writing is just fine." Maybe your writing is fine, but could it be better? It's been my experience that most college students believe they're excellent writers when, in fact, less than a third truly excel at the skill. Yes, that sounds harsh. I am not saying that two-thirds of college students fail at writing, rather, that most college students could use help—some of it significant—with their writing. Although a few great writers are born, most are made, and there is no better way to improve your writing than by reading up on how to improve your ability and then practicing it in your papers.

Writing in the Era of Texting

Again, I can hear some of you complaining. "Come on, you're being so 'old school.' Maybe perfect grammar mattered when you were in school, but with the Internet, texting, and tweeting, the new generation of writers uses a more casual style." Ah, but that confuses style with comprehension. Unless told otherwise by your professors or listed in the instructions for a paper, you should feel free to use any writing style that you prefer. If you want to write in the first person instead of the supposedly "objective" third person, go right ahead. If you want to structure your English paper as a letter back to Shakespeare, telling him why you're disappointed with one his plays, your teacher should applaud your creativity. But these stylistic choices are distinct from writing in clear prose so the reader understands what you are trying to say. Use "effect" when you mean "affect," and the reader will not be able to follow the argument. Misplace a modifier and your instructor may not appreciate the extent of your critique. Good writing matters, if only to be understood.

But there is also an issue of respect. If you treat a college paper as breezily as you would a text to your friends, you are telling your professor that you did not think the assignment worthy of your time. Maybe that's the case, but do you really want to risk a bad grade because you could not be bothered to write out the word "okay" and instead used the shorthand "k"? Of course, English evolves, which is why new words are added to the dictionary each year. But taking the time to spell out words completely—heck, to use words instead of the symbols from your cell phone—and write in full sentences never goes out of style, at least not if you're writing a college paper.

I realize I am shouting into the wind here, but you need to remember that in college we're teaching a different, more serious kind of writing. Think of it as writing for authority. Whether it's for a college course or a later assignment in your chosen career, you simply have to learn how to write satisfactorily if you expect to succeed. Ask your parents if they have ever seen a sales report that begins, "Dude, our product is so bogus it's almost a joke. But check it out, our customers are so lame they'll take it. LOL." An employee like this would soon find himself looking for a new job.

That is not what you want. The colleague you should aim to be, the applicant you'll want to emulate, and the student you should work at becoming is the one who knows how to present herself as a respectful, earnest, and stimulating communicator, the "go-to person" when there is an important assignment to be completed. This is where good writing comes in, for it's been my experience that good writers are good thinkers. In fact, I have yet to come across a good writer who did not also reason well. I have met many fine thinkers who could not convey their ideas effectively on paper, but the inverse is not true. Effective writing helps to improve your thinking and reasoning so that you can keep more ideas in your mind at one time and in a distinct and logical order. So by working on your writing you are also helping yourself to comprehend and analyze material in other ways.

Good Writers Can Be Made

If you are not already a good writer, do not fret. Good writing can be developed if the student is committed to practice. Your composition courses are excellent opportunities for growth, but so are other "topical" courses if you are willing to work with your instructor. Most professors are delighted to see a student stop by at various stages of a paper to consult on outlines or parts of a draft. In some classes you may even be required to turn in a rough draft of a larger paper so that your instructor can go over your writing with you while there is still plenty of time for revision and editing.

In other cases, however, your writing may need more work than an instructor can be expected to provide in the classroom or during office hours. Perhaps your writing is not yet up to college-level standards. Maybe English is not your native language. In those cases, most colleges have writing centers with skilled assistants and tutors to provide you the kind of individualized attention you need. I discuss those resources at greater length in the next chapter and strongly urge you to take advantage of them if you need to, or even if you think it would be useful to get extra assistance in improving your writing. There is no shame in acknowledging that you're having difficulty with college-level writing. The real problem is when you do not take strong and timely steps to address those troubles.

Citation and Plagiarism

According to a report from Carnegie Mellon University, the current generation of students was "raised with the Internet, where information flows without a defined sense of intellectual ownership." As a result, you "may or may not grasp the concept of intellectual property, understand fully what plagiarism is, or recognize why universities consider plagiarism a serious offense."[12] Plagiarism is indeed a serious offense, because it contradicts the very purpose of scholarship. Scholars rise or fall within academe on the basis of their research and ideas. Frankly, we have no other currency (besides our ability to teach, which is nowhere near as well compensated). It is the originality of our ideas and the quality of our research projects and findings that establish our place within our profession.

In academe, our words are our property. Just as you would not walk into a bank and take bags of money from the vault, no right-thinking scholar would ever copy someone else's words or ideas and pass them off as his own. Although we often reference or employ other people's work in our own, we are very careful to credit them, as, for example, when one team of researchers seeks to build on the prior findings of other groups. Think of the polio vaccine. Although Albert Sabin and Jonas Salk raced one another to discover a cure to this once-deadly disease, even Sabin, who created the oral vaccine, would have acknowledged that Salk got there first and that the information obtained from Salk's injectable vaccine proved useful in producing an oral vaccine.

The Rules of Referencing

When enrolling as a college student, you, too, become bound by these norms. We certainly expect you to read from and employ others' research; that is essential to learning. But in doing so, you will be held to the rules of referencing. Essentially, there are two, which you need to commit to memory. First, any time you quote from the work of another, you must use quotation marks and include a citation to the original source. This is the simplest rule of the two to understand. If you were to write in a paper, "To be or not to be, that is the question," you would have to cite to Shakespeare's play *Hamlet*, which is where this notable expression originated.[13]

The second rule is more subtle. Any time you paraphrase the work of another or make a point that is not common knowledge and that you learned from another source, you must note the original source in the paper. For example, if you were to say that voters in 2006 tossed out Republican incumbents and in 2010 did the same to Democrats, because they were worried that the country was on the wrong track, you would need to cite a source for this point, since you were presumably unaware of this fact until you did your research. You do not need to use quotation marks for the passage (unless you are directly quoting from the original source), but even paraphrasing requires a citation, as the electoral explanation would not be your original idea.

Referencing Style

Depending on your professor and the field in which you are writing the paper, you may have several options for citation style. Some of the most common come from the American Psychological Association, the Modern Language Association, the American Medical Association, the legal community, this publisher—the University of Chicago Press—and even a modification to it, Turabian. With the exception of legal citations, most citation styles permit you to place a short parenthetical directly into the text of your paper to cite an author's name so long as you then include a bibliography at the end of your paper that lists all of the sources cited. Unless you are a law student—which should still be a few years off—you should *not* be using footnotes to cite your sources. In fact, footnote citation is often a red flag for instructors, who see it as the mark of a student trying to add pages to a paper without actually including any substantive text.

Let me give an example to illustrate the two rules of referencing. Suppose you read a recent article from Jane Smith in which she said on page 164, "The prison population is down 30 percent since 1980." In a paper on prison policy in the U.S., you could use this material one of two ways, either as a direct quote or for general support. The citations for each would look as follows:

Direct quotation: The corrections system is not as crowded as it used to be; in fact "the prison population is down 30 percent since 1980" (Smith 2011, 164). Wardens, then, must be concerned about keeping their jobs.

Paraphrasing: The corrections system is not as crowded as it used to be, as prison populations are dropping (Smith 2011). Wardens, then, must be concerned about keeping their jobs.

Then under either approach, you would provide the full citation for the article in the bibliography:

Smith, Jane. 2011. "Prison Populations." *Law and Social Inquiry* 32:158–75.

For more information on citations and bibliographies, you should consult a grammar book, talk to your professor, or visit your school's writing center. I cannot emphasize enough how important it is to properly cite others' publications that you use in your own writing. To transgress this rule is to invite a very serious punishment.

Stealth Plagiarism

There is a type of plagiarism that you may not even realize counts. If you attempt to submit a paper for more than one class, several schools will consider that a violation of their academic integrity policies. I recognize it may seem odd to call this plagiarism—after all, how can you be charged with copying from yourself? But the purpose of academic honesty and anti-plagiarism policies is to ensure that the work you submit in your classes is original and that you properly cite any material you did not dream up on your own for that assignment.

Technically, then, if you submit a paper from your history class for an assignment in an English class, the English paper is not original and may run afoul of your school's academic integrity policy. Some of these policies have exceptions that permit dual submission with the permission of instructors from both classes. In those instances it is crucial to get permission well ahead of the due dates so that you can undertake a separate, second paper if the professors will not grant your request. To blow them off, however, and submit the same paper twice is to play a needless game of academic roulette.

Plagiarism Is Easily Detectable

I have seen too many students over the years risk a plagiarism charge. It really is a silly and brainless exercise, because the vast majority of plagiarism cases are easily discovered. Just as students can use the Internet to search for passages to pass off as their own, professors, too, can hunt down those same phrases. In many cases, a student who is not an especially good writer will stick an uncited passage into his paper that doesn't match in tone or style. This immediately raises our suspicions and compels us to go find the original source, which we almost always do. (Remember, it's our job to conduct research. You're only baiting us if you try this tactic.) Some schools have even employed software programs like Turnitin, which runs students' electronically submitted papers through a massive search engine to match text from the paper with similar phrases available online, in journals, or in books. Matched but uncited text is a red flag for plagiarism.

Purchased Papers

Other students have attempted to purchase or "borrow" papers written by others. There is no dearth of online services, with hustlers willing to take your cash in exchange for a paper to be passed off as your own.[14] Putting aside the ethics of these services (and I hope you recognize they are horribly unethical), you are taking three risks in using them. First, there is no guarantee that they will actually deliver the paper on time. Imagine spending upwards of $300 on a paper only to find that someone has taken your cash and vanished.

Second, you have no assurance about the quality of the final product. Let's say, for example, that you're a C student and that you are looking for a B-or-higher paper to improve your course grade. The reality is that most of the papers you can purchase on the Internet are of fair-to-poor quality, meaning that your grade is likely to suffer even if your professor does not discover the plagiarism.

Finally, many of the purchased papers seem to sound alike, meaning that it is relatively easy for a professor to do a search and find passages from the paper floating around the Internet. I can remember confronting a student over what appeared to be a purchased paper, asking him about an obscure, uncited expression in the paper that "mysteriously" had multiple hits when I checked it on the Internet. When challenged about how "his" expression could have appeared in several papers before him, he offered the howler of an excuse of "random chance."[15] (In the end, the university's honor committee found him guilty of plagiarism.)

Editing Assistance

I have been asked before where the line exists between editing assistance on a paper and plagiarism. It's a good question. Suppose you share a copy of your paper with your mom, who is an exceptional writer, and she sends back several suggested edits for your paper. If you incorporate all of those changes, have you violated your school's plagiarism policy by, essentially, turning in the work of your mom? The answer is no, provided you meet two criteria.

First, that early draft must have been your own work. If you have the ultimate in helicopter parents who offers to write the first draft of your school papers, then not only do you need to start enforcing limits but you also have committed plagiarism. Second, it must be your judgment about which edits to incorporate into your draft. Even the best writers will share manuscripts with outsider reviewers and editors for recommended improvements, but it is always the decision of the original author about which recommendations to follow. The same should be true for your papers. Feel free to show your drafts to anyone who is willing to help, but remember that it must be your call on the eventual presentation or you will risk plagiarism.

Don't Insult Your Professors by Plagiarizing

Like many of my colleagues, I take plagiarism very personally. It's not simply an affront to academic integrity; at some level plagiarism is also an insult to your professor's intelligence. Students who attempt to cheat are essentially issuing a two-pronged insult to their professors: not only that they don't care enough about the class to do their own work, but also that they don't think the professor is deft enough to figure out they're cheating. Even if a student doesn't care about a class, we do—and believe me, when we catch a student who has knowingly plagiarized, few of us want to go easy on him. In fact, the penalties from a plagiarism charge can be quite severe—ranging from academic probation and a notation on your transcript for an inadvertent, initial act to expulsion from the school over serious or multiple charges. These penalties have a way of following you throughout life. Try explaining to the admissions committee of a graduate program why you are a good risk as an applicant if you previously have been caught cheating on academic assignments. Or try passing an FBI background check when the investigators learn you were suspended for plagiarism. Even in a country that loves redemption stories, there is no point putting yourself in the position of having to explain why you cheated.

Fortunately, plagiarism is not the norm at most schools, and the vast majority of students does an honest job of writing papers. Whether those papers are well written is, of course, another story. But if you follow the advice in this chapter, you will maximize your chances of both doing solid work and earning a good grade on your written assignments. I cannot guarantee you an A—and, frankly, except at schools with outrageous grade inflation no one can—but it really is possible for most students to earn good grades on their papers. The trick is planning out enough time to do a thorough job and taking advantage of all the resources available to you. Meet with your instructors early in the research process to discuss your assignment; show them outlines and early drafts if they will read them; consult good writers, including the assistants at your school's writing center; and remember to allow plenty of time to revise and edit your writing. The Shakespeares of the world may be born, but the rest of us can train ourselves to become respectable writers.

6

SPECIAL CIRCUMSTANCES

In a perfect world, you would breeze through college in four years without a bump. You would remain fit and healthy, each of your classes would go swimmingly, and you would suffer no personal setbacks. Although you're unlikely to experience major problems during your time with us, college life, like life in general, never goes perfectly. You may face an especially difficult but required course, a sporting meet may conflict with a paper deadline, or you may get a nasty flu. Even if you steer clear of these challenges, you must still decide what to do with your life after college, a perplexing if not worrisome prospect for many students. Whatever the worry, this chapter will help you to address any stumbling blocks when things at college don't go exactly according to plan. The good news is that almost all of these challenges can be handled if you address them head-on. Most schools are designed to serve the needs of their students. But you have to be willing to acknowledge when you're having difficulty and seek and accept help. This chapter explains how you can accomplish that.

Academic Problems

College classes are supposed to be challenging, but challenging does not mean impossible. If you find a course to be unintelligible, if you see that you're falling significantly behind or that your grade continues to drop, you need to take action. Start with your professor or teaching assistant; make an appointment to discuss your difficulty with the class. For many students, the solution is regular attendance at office hours, where an instructor can help answer questions or explain the material in greater detail. For other students, though, the problems may run deeper, reflecting either a personal problem, a learning disability, or a skills deficiency.

Academic Skills

I realize that last item may sound like an oxymoron to some readers. How is it that a school would admit students who lack some of the necessary academic skills to handle the work? The answer is complicated. In many situations, students are perfectly capable but have difficulty with one area of study. In my case, for example, geometric or "right-brain" thinking is especially hard. If I were to take a geometry class at this point in my life, I'm sure I would want a tutor. In other cases, students may test well on standardized or multiple-choice exams but lack good writing skills. The SAT and ACT exams have tried to address this possible incongruity by adding a written portion, although not all schools require the writing test for admission. Hence, a smart student who has not been challenged to write well in high school could presumably find his way to college, where he would need remedial instruction in composition.

There has been a great deal of discussion and consternation in academic circles about the "dumbing down" of high school education and the resulting problems it provides for colleges that potentially face a less-qualified applicant pool. The most prestigious institutions can ignore this dilemma by accepting only the cream of the high school crop, but for many other colleges the choice isn't so simple. Schools that rely heavily on tuition dollars to cover their expenses may be willing to provide the necessary remedial courses in order to fill an entering class.

I confess that I come down on the side of those who believe that remedial instruction should not be necessary at a four-year college, and, indeed, I have taught several students over the years who began at a community college to strengthen their basic academic skills before transferring to a four-year institution. That is a well-worn and advisable path that gives students a chance to fine-tune their analytical and writing skills before tacking the more intensive work load of a four-year college.

But one can be a top high school graduate with good SAT scores and still have academic difficulties in college. Perhaps your writing or reading skills need improvement. Maybe you're having trouble understanding what is asked of you in assignments. Fortunately, most colleges have a learning-skills program or a writing center. These are wonderful resources that provide supplementary classes, peer tutoring, and editing services to students who could benefit from extra instruction or assistance. I have seen these programs do great work, helping students whose writing was substandard rise to the level of respectable. For students who "skated by" in high school on the basis of raw intellect, a learning-skills program can help to teach the process of active reading and note taking and can coach them in the process of studying for an exam. Over the years, I have referred many students to such programs—not because I was angry with or disappointed in them, but because I could see that they would benefit from the extra instruction.

The key is to recognize the problem as it is happening, a process, I know, that is easier said than done. Most people don't like to acknowledge they're having difficulties, especially when they're not sure what help is available. At a small liberal arts school, your professors may be the first to approach you, having noticed difficulties you are having in class or on assignments. At larger schools where big lecture classes make it less likely that your instructors recognize you by name, you may have to make the initial diagnosis. Do you find it difficult to follow what your instructor is saying in class? Do the examples or explanations he offers make little sense? Are you unable to synthesize your notes or study effectively for a test? Is writing papers extremely difficult? Has it gotten to the point where you're beginning to avoid your schoolwork out of frustration or confusion? More distressing, have you received tests or papers back with grades of Ds or Fs?

If any of these statements apply to you, make an appointment to talk to your instructor during office hours. Describe to him exactly what you're experiencing, and repeat these three crucial words: "I need help." I cannot think of a professor who is unwilling to provide extra assistance to a student who acknowledges he is having difficulty and is willing to put in extra time to address the situation. Your instructor may set up regular appointments for you to come to office hours for supplemental instruction; she may refer you to the teaching assistant or a tutor for assistance; or she may contact the learning skills or writing center and help you make a diagnostic appointment. Of course, you must be willing to follow through and participate in the extra sessions, but there is absolutely no reason to suffer in silence on your own. As I have said earlier in this book, every student who has been admitted to college ought to be able to graduate with a reasonable GPA. This does not mean straight As, or even Bs, but colleges are set up to ensure students have the resources to tackle the material and graduate. That depends, though, on student initiative. There is no shame in experiencing difficulty with your classes or assignments. The real disgrace is ignoring the signs of trouble and failing to take corrective action.

Learning Disabilities

Colleges and universities have gotten better over the last twenty years in recognizing and accommodating students' learning disabilities. No longer are such students shunted aside as substandard scholars. Today, most schools are enlightened enough to recognize that, with appropriate accommodations, many smart but disabled students can excel at college.

Unlike in primary or secondary schools, colleges are not required to provide specialized instruction for disabled students. Instead, schools offer what are known as reasonable accommodations. If a student has attention deficit hyperactivity disorder (ADHD) and needs a quiet room and more time on an exam, these can be provided. Similarly, a student who has a physical disability, say deafness, can request that a school provide a sign-language interpreter in her classes. Each of these accommodations is considered reasonable and necessary.

A school's response to student disabilities is governed by federal statute—the Americans with Disabilities Act—so as you might imagine, most schools follow a formal and unwavering process in considering students' disabilities. A professor is not permitted to evaluate a student's request for accommodations on his own. That is an ironclad rule at most schools, an imperative that some students may fail to appreciate. Instead, they will approach their instructors on their own, asking for extra time or some other uncomplicated accommodation for an exam or paper. Although I understand the motivation to keep things simple and informal, please understand that your professors are not trying to be unsympathetic in referring you or your classmates to the school's disability services office. Not only must a school confirm a student's disability, but its response and accommodations for the student must be consistent. There are countless court judgments in favor of aggrieved students whose disabilities were accommodated by some of their professors and dismissed by others. It's an expensive proposition for schools to lose these cases, so smart institutions put procedures in place to address the needs of students with disabilities.

If you are a student with a disability of any kind, whether physical, mental, or learning, contact your school's disability services office as soon as you decide to enroll. There is no reason to try to "tough it out" with a diagnosed disability when a reasonable accommodation could help you to excel. Be prepared to provide sufficient proof from your doctor, counselor, or previous school to establish the disability, along with a list of recommended accommodations. Once your school certifies the disability, it will likely create a form for you to share with your professors explaining the nature of your disability and outlining the accommodations that instructors must make for you. Do not be shy in seeking these accommodations. They are your right under law, and you more than deserve them. I have no doubt that your disability has inconvenienced you in many ways over the years. Although accommodations cannot make up for the disability, they reflect your school's recognition that you are perfectly capable of doing college level work and that with the appropriate accommodations you will be on the same playing field as your classmates.

Health and Family Emergencies

An academic study indicates that grandparents die disproportionately between Thanksgiving and Christmas.[1] Or, at least that is what college students seem to tell their professors. Astonishingly, the grandparents of these students appeared to pass away in large numbers just as their grandchildren were busy completing their term papers or studying for finals. I hate to sound so cynical, but I have seen any number of fake excuses for missed assignments. It has gotten to the point where I now ask students for proof of the family emergency they claim. I've had students bring copies of plane tickets, news stories, even funeral programs to substantiate their stories. Mind you, I always provide a dispensation for students in times of emergency, but the reports must be real.

Should an emergency strike you—and I very much hope it does not—any professor with an ounce of decency will go out of his way to accommodate you. If you have to travel to a funeral, take time off to heal, or even, as I have seen firsthand, depart class because your partner is going into labor, your instructor can help you to adapt to the situation. If there is any advice I can leave you with for these situations it is to be up front and proactive with your instructors about the circumstances. If you're likely to be called home to see a terminally ill relative, let your professor know as soon as possible. If you're facing misdemeanor charges and may be spending a few days with the local authorities (it has happened), tell your teachers before you're absent.

Why the advance notice? So you can begin planning to make up work before you're gone. Perhaps your instructor can give you advance homework or reading assignments or share upcoming deadlines with you. Maybe she'll invite you to office hours to provide specialized instruction for the classes you will miss. Or she can adjust paper or exam deadlines so you don't add to your stress while worrying about how you will make up the missing assignments. Make sure you give the professor the whole story, too, so she can assess how deserving your request is. I understand that you may be embarrassed about particular situations—a parent who will be arraigned in court, a personal medical procedure that you are facing—but the more you can brief your professor about your situation the better she will understand why you should be offered dispensation.

If the situation is especially dire and you'll have to be absent from campus for two weeks or more, go see your dean of students or student services staff to inquire about other options. Depending on how far you are into the semester, some schools will permit you to elect an incomplete in the class, thereby allowing you several months to make up the coursework. Or you may want to withdraw from your classes for the affected semester. I know this is usually an unappealing option, but it also may be the best opportunity to save your GPA. If, for example, you learn in the second week of the term that you need an immediate operation with a six-week recuperation period, you're better off withdrawing from classes and returning in the next term when you're at full strength. If the withdrawal is for an emergency and not because you simply changed your mind about attending the school, most colleges will work with you in preserving your financial aid package.

Counseling

Fortunately, the vast majority of college students will never face the kind of dire emergency that warrants a temporary withdrawal from school. But, as in the rest of life, most students will encounter some painful periods at college. It goes with the territory. As you're coming into your own and becoming an adult, you'll be facing some novel pressures and growing pains. Even if you've spent considerable time away from home before, most students get homesick at some point. It can be stressful to learn how to navigate the daily responsibilities of life on your own—getting yourself up and off to class without anyone to prod you; handling your own laundry, banking, and in some situations cooking; learning how to manage your time, especially when there are so many attractive distractions; and, speaking of attraction, navigating the waters of college hookups and, eventually, relationships.

If you feel your anxiety rising or sense a slide toward depression, the best thing you can do for yourself is to seek help. Most schools maintain a counseling center with trained staff to help you. If the situation is especially dire, student health services can even prescribe medication. The key is to go, even if you're not sure you should. There is no embarrassment is admitting times are tough; lasting damage comes only if you let an emotional open wound continue to seep, in the end affecting not only your mood and well-being but also your academic performance. There is a strong link between your mood and coursework, which makes sense if you think about it. If you're panicked, it will be difficult to focus, since your mind will be spinning about what might go wrong. Similarly, anyone who has been depressed can tell you that it is virtually impossible to summon the mental energy necessary to do any classwork while caught in a downward spiral. Since several forms of mental illness tend to emerge in the eighteen-to-twenty-four-year age range, know that you are not alone if you are having difficulties.

I know it can be difficult to recognize when it's time to seek additional help. Breaking up with your high school girlfriend can be very painful, but this may not necessitate extra support beyond the shoulder of a sympathetic friend. Even so, I urge you to err on the side of caution. There is the rare person among us who would not benefit from counseling or psychological support. Moreover, the slide from mild worry to extreme anxiety or from disappointment to depression can be fast, especially if coupled with alcohol or drug dependency.

Substance Abuse

Ah, alcohol and drugs. If there is one problem that probably lays low the greatest number of college students it is the misuse of these substances. I won't lie and claim that drinking ages are enforced on college campuses. Except at a small number of (largely religious) institutions, alcohol flows as freely in the dorms and fraternity and sorority houses as at the local bars, and alcohol abuse is closely connected to a host of other campus ills, including vandalism and even date rape. Marijuana and, to a lesser extent, more serious drugs are usually available too. But their availability hardly means that college is a debauched bender. Most college students drink in moderation, and, in fact, fewer than half have ever tried marijuana.[2]

If students begin to slip into dependency, most school do a good job of providing assistance, but that only happens if college officials are aware of the difficulties. It's not as if the student services staff have specialized radar that will alert them when students are anxious, depressed, or abusing drugs. If you have having trouble, or if you know of someone who is, it is imperative that you flash even a small sign to someone—anyone—on campus who can help. If you're living in the dorms, approach your resident advisor; send an e-mail to an academic advisor; stop by to see the student services staff; or even better, walk yourself over to the counseling center and simply say, "I think I could use some help." They will take it from there.

You may have noticed that I didn't mention your professors. We will certainly refer any student in need to the counseling department, and in some cases we'll even walk with you over to the center. But we are not trained counselors, and we are often cautioned to remember our limits. As I've said repeatedly in this book, we really do want the best for you; that's why we're in this profession. We enjoy teaching you, chatting with you before and after class, and offering academic, professional, and occasionally personal advice. In several cases, we establish lifelong friendships with students. But we're not in a position to offer counseling, especially when students are hurting psychologically. So if you find your professor referring you to the counseling center, please understand that the teacher is not trying to put you off; rather, he or she is truly concerned about your best interests.

Grade Appeals

Let's say you have followed all of my advice up to this point—you have been an active reader, you have gone to class and taken and synthesized your notes, you have prepared effectively for tests and left yourself enough time to complete your papers—and yet you still end up with a course grade that disappoints you. Without knowing the course or your performance, the truth may be that the grade, however much lower than you would prefer, is an accurate reflection of your mastery of the subject. I understand that may not be what you want to hear, but intuitively I suspect you recognize that each of us has our strengths and weaknesses. You may excel at math or science and have greater difficulties with English or European history. So long as you are confident that you did your best under the circumstances, then you should take pride in your accomplishment no matter what the final grade may be.

In some cases, however, your course grade may not be an accurate assessment of your performance in the class. Perhaps your professor miscalculated the points on an exam or did not read the back page of your blue book. Maybe the instructor misunderstood your argument in a paper and did not see that it was responsive to the question asked. Professors are people too, and we occasionally make mistakes in grading.

If you suspect an error, your first step should be to schedule a time to talk with your professor in a constructive and professional manner. Do not attempt to pull the instructor aside before or after class when she is likely rushed and unable to devote the proper attention to your question. Instead, come to office hours or e-mail her and ask for a short appointment. Approach your instructor calmly, without accusation or defensiveness. Ultimately, you are trying to convince your professor that she made an error, and it is the rare person among us who responds well to name-calling or anger. Come prepared with the assignment or grading rubric and compare those to the relevant sections from your paper or exam. Then explain to your professor why you believe your submission meets the requirements and how or why the error in grading was made. A good professor will hear you out and, if your case is convincing and her error plain, make the correction. None of us has any interest in denying you the credit you deserve.

Keep in mind, though, that professors can be inundated with students challenging their grades. Most often, this happens at the end of a semester when final grades are to be submitted and some students come face-to-face with the results of their inattention during the term. So if at first your professor is skeptical about your claim, please understand that she may be fending off a large number of "grade grubbers."

In some cases, however, you may be up against an unreasonable instructor, and no matter how persuasive your arguments, you may still get a cold shoulder. In those cases, you may want to consider invoking your college's grade appeals process. Most schools usually have such a policy, which establishes a procedure for formally appealing a final course grade. I should caution you that these processes can take up to a semester to complete and are, in fact, tilted to the instructor who gave you the grade. This does not mean that the process is biased or that you have no chance in appealing. Rather, if the dispute comes down to your take on a particular assignment and your instructor's evaluation of the same, the appeals committee will likely defer to the judgment of your teacher, who is presumed to be more knowledgeable about the subject. Depending on your school, the appeals process may require that you return to your instructor one more time and attempt to resolve the matter, but in all likelihood your claim will be taken before a group of professors from the instructor's home department and then on to the department chair or dean. You will have an opportunity to explain your appeal, and the committee will hear from the instructor, too. Shortly thereafter, a decision will be made.

If this sounds like a process designed to discourage appeals, it is, but again, not out of some grand conspiracy to deny you the appropriate grade. Rather, it reflects the fact that some students will protest any grade that disappoints them, regardless of whether it was deserved. Of course, the easiest way to avoid a contested grade is to keep in regular touch with your instructor during the semester, come to office hours as you're studying for exams, and submit early drafts of your papers for review and comment. That way, your professor will be up-to-date on your progress, and you will have multiple opportunities to clear up any ambiguities on assignments before they are due. Moreover, by building a reserve of goodwill with your professor by your obvious interest in the class, you will be in a much better position to question any grades that you find doubtful.

The Student Athlete

For those of you who follow college athletics, you may note that the NCAA always refers to college athletes as "student-athletes." Never athletes or athlete-students. "Student" always comes first in the NCAA's designation. Although I understand doubts about the term's application to Division I, big-time college sports[3]—one need only examine the graduation rates of men's basketball players in top-ten programs—the vast majority of college students who also play a sport are truly students first. This is undoubtedly the case for student-athletes at smaller Division III schools that don't provide athletic scholarships, but it's also largely true for students on athletic scholarship at other institutions. If a student cannot maintain an acceptable GPA, his playing days are numbered.

If you play a sport while attending college, you know the tremendous demands on your time. During season, you often must arise hours earlier than your classmates for a morning workout, then attend classes, participate in afternoon practice, and fit in time for studying before heading to bed, only to begin the process the next morning. You may have to miss classes or exams to attend a game or tournament, and even in the off-season you're expected to appear for practice or strength training on a regular basis. To be sure, the regimen I've just described applies more often to those sports that offer a professional alternative, but it's not just football, basketball, and baseball I have in mind. Even sports and schools that are far less competitive demand a significant time commitment from their student-athletes.

If you are one of these students, you'll need to make peace from the beginning that your sport will likely crowd out time for a relaxing social life. There simply aren't enough hours in the day (or night). If this is going to nag at you, if you suspect you will feel bitter turning down invitations for a Thursday night movie, then think again about participating in the sport. I'm not saying that you will have to throw away a social life. Saturday night—especially after a big game—still beckons. But if you expect to achieve peak performance on the field and in the classroom, then you will have to be especially disciplined.

Depending on your school and sport, the athletic department may schedule, supervise, and even support your studying. This is especially true of big-time sports programs, where schools are concerned about keeping star athletes academically eligible and worry about reporting graduation rates to the NCAA. More often, it is up to the student-athletes to stay current on classwork even as they practice and perform on the field. The athletic department may monitor your academic performance—seeking interim progress reports from your professors—but ultimately the responsibility is yours. No one will step in unless you're having problems.

Most faculty are unaware they have athletes in the classroom unless they are told by the students themselves. To be sure, some student-athletes stand out because of their height or build, but most of the time we would be hard pressed to identify, say, a soccer forward unless told. For the student-athlete, this means that faculty will not automatically make accommodations to your schedule or needs. From our perspective at the front of the classroom, student-athletes look like anyone else in the course and are treated the same. Frankly, this is the way it ought to be. That a student is committed to baseball is no more important to the school's atmosphere than another student who devotes similar hours to editing the daily paper. Ultimately, you need to perform in the classroom regardless of your extracurricular activities, or else you will find your days on campus numbered.

There are, however, two areas in which faculty often will make dispensations for student-athletes. At many schools, professors are told to schedule make-up exams if students must be absent to participate in a sanctioned athletic event. Most often, students need to leave campus early on a particular day to travel to a game at another school. If the travel corresponds with an exam, then instructors are asked to provide a make-up opportunity for the athletes. This is part of our job, and we'll offer the accommodation.

But keep in mind that it is the student's responsibility to provide us advance notice. Many coaches distribute a schedule of games to the team at the beginning of a season and ask that the students give copies to their professors—sometimes with a required signature to prove that the instructors were notified. Of course, schedules can change, especially as a team advances through a postseason tournament, but ultimately, it is the responsibility of the student to keep his or her professor notified so that make-ups can be arranged. Note, however, that while exams will be rescheduled if a student cannot be present, the deadlines for other assignments may not be moved. If you have known about a term paper for weeks, your professor may prove unsympathetic when asked to extend the deadline simply because your crew team advanced an extra day or two in a regatta.

The other area in which professors may offer accommodations or even intervene is with a student-athlete's classroom performance. Many instructors appreciate the extra demands on an athlete and may even admire the dedication students show by balancing a sport with classes. Should a student-athlete fall behind on assignments during his or her season, some professors may be open to requests to postpone assignments. Most often, the student will have to initiate the conversation, but if the student is otherwise attending class and putting in a good effort, the instructor may be sympathetic.

The more difficult situation is if the student begins to fall behind because she is not following the course content. Sometimes this happens because the student is unable to devote sufficient time to her studies during her sport's season, which is one reason why some coaches recommend that athletes take a lighter academic load when in season. If you play lacrosse, for example, you might want to take three, rather than four, classes in the spring semester and make up the extra class in the summer or in a later term.

Other times, however, student-athletes falter because they are insufficiently prepared for a course. I realize I'm treading on delicate sands here. I suspect we're all familiar with the stereotype of the "dumb jock"—the athlete who doesn't measure up academically but was admitted because a coach needs a star quarterback, forward, or pitcher. These students do exist, and I've taught them. But if my experience is a guide, most athletes have the same level of intelligence and drive as other "typical" students. To some extent, they have to if they want to balance school with sports. For that matter, most student-athletes will not make their sport a career and thus have to concentrate on their studies for good opportunities after graduation.

Still, like their classmates, student-athletes may find themselves overwhelmed, lost, or falling behind in a class. If this describes you, approach the situation much as I've advised students in general: be proactive. Approach your professor and admit the problem. Describe the difficulties you're having and ask for advice. Consider telling your coach as well. Depending on your school and sport, the athletic department may provide tutors to help navigate your way out of confusion. In fact, in the big "revenue sports," your coach may even be aware of your academic difficulties before you are, as professors and the coaching staff often communicate regularly about the performance of top athletes.

At smaller schools or in less organized sports, the responsibility to seek help will rest more squarely on the student-athlete's shoulders, but even in these situations students will have access to their college's learning-skills center. If this situation describes you, ask your professor to make a referral. Although an instructor's intervention is not needed to seek help from the resource center, the overture will provide an additional aid, ensuring that you move to the top of the queue and that the tutors are already aware of your difficulties when you set foot in the office. You also should make a point of attending your instructor's office hours on a regular basis. If these conflict with your sport's schedule, make appointments to visit at alternate times. There really is no better alternative than one-on-one instruction from your professor. In addition to answering your questions, the interactions should help you to understand which topics your instructor considers most important for tests and quizzes.

Just keep in mind that your professor must balance the extra time he spends with you with his responsibilities to your classmates. If your difficulties are significant, he may refer you to the learning-skills center for remedial instruction and recommend that you retake his course after you have improved your more basic academic skills. Or he may coordinate his efforts with a teaching assistant or even a tutor provided by the athletic department. Don't be put out if he involves others. Ultimately, if you are proactive and acknowledge your difficulties—and, most importantly, if you are truly willing to put in the effort to address those troubles—your professor should be willing to help. He may even quarterback that team. Unlike your coach, though, he has no greater interest in your academic success than that of your classmates. So if you're having problems in class, it will be up to you to approach him, not necessarily the other way around.

Postgraduation

Eventually, your days with us at college will draw to a close, and, even if you have mixed feelings about leaving the cocoon of campus, it will be time for you to move on to other adventures. Your faculty, too, will bid you goodbye with a variety of emotions. Like you, we take pride in your accomplishments and are pleased to see you earn the diploma. And of course, there is a bit of selfish personal pride in accomplishing *our* goal of graduating another class. But just as you hopefully have developed ties to your alma mater, we often have established a close professional connection to the school's future alumni—you! So don't be surprised if, on graduation day, you encounter more than one of your professors who greets you or your family with a misty eye or two. If you have been a good student, trying your best, joining in class discussions, and coming to office hours, we'll be sad to see you go.

But go you must, and it's your college's job to help prepare you for what lies ahead. Essentially, you have five options upon graduation: further graduate study, a fellowship, an entry-level career position, coasting with odd jobs, or unemployment. I presume that none of us wishes for the last option. Even if your parents will let you live at home in their basement while you spend countless hours playing video games, I'm confident that this would not be their dream for you after four years and thousands of dollars of college. I suspect it's not your ideal vision either.

More and more, I see recent graduates coasting for several years after college as they work temporary or hourly positions. Some of this plight is due to a national economy that has yet to open up a sufficient number of well-paying entry-level jobs. But some, too, is the result of what sociologists call "delayed adolescence." Whereas your grandparents' generation was expected to get married in their early twenties and start a family shortly thereafter, today the average age of marriage is approaching twenty-seven. The result is a span of several years after college in which some graduates feel rudderless. They're no longer children but don't yet feel like adults, and as a result they don't take steps to begin the kind of career that would bring them further fulfillment— and a higher and more permanent salary—in the years ahead.

I have no problem with college grads taking a year or two after college to "play," if you will. In fact, I have a brother who did so, and he is the envy of his friends for having spent a year after college in Aspen as a ski bum, working as a short-order cook at night and skiing all day. Today, he is a computer professional with two master's degrees, three children, and a mortgage; in fact, he met his wife in Aspen while she was there taking a year off as well. That may not be your ideal vision, but the point remains: there is nothing wrong with, and perhaps lots to be gained from, taking a year or so to float following graduation while you pursue a vocational or avocational interest and think through your next steps. Travel through Europe while you aren't responsible for anyone other than yourself; go spend the year in New Zealand. Whatever speaks to you, *provided, however*, that you are both able to support yourself and are deliberately making the choice. If your parents have already paid for your education, it's patently unfair to expect that they will continue to support your "lifestyle" after graduation; and, if you have student loans from your college days, those lenders are unlikely to wait a year or more while you find sufficient employment to begin repaying your debt.

But it's more than being able to afford life after graduation. I find that too many students fail to make deliberate postcollege plans because the prospect is scary. I get that. It's stressful to confront the reality that college will come to a close and that soon you will be responsible for your own decisions. But I also suspect that some students make the situation worse for themselves by imagining that they are making decisions about "the rest of their lives." In truth, most career decisions—and certainly the first few after college—don't have permanent consequences. If you try one path and find that, after a few years, it's not what you wanted, you can always change. I'm the prime example—a former lawyer, human rights activist, and campaign worker who is now a professor. Or, consider two of my son's former middle school teachers, one of whom was an FBI agent and the other a computer programmer for a bank, both of whom decided after a few years to enter teaching and are excellent at their new profession.

If I keep saying it in this book, it's only because the statement is true: there is not a single, linear path toward career or personal satisfaction. At twenty-one, you shouldn't know what you'll want to do two decades in the future. So take the pressure off yourself and begin imaging what you want to do now or next, not what you ought to be doing eventually. As I have found time and again among the students I have taught, those who have had the most fulfilling professional lives take one opportunity at a time, work at it fully while learning as much as they can from the position, and then make a move when they're ready. Like all successful professionals, they plan ahead, but they limit themselves to two central questions: 1) What do I want to do, learn, or experience next? 2) What will it take to get there? They're not focused on three steps down the road, nor are they holding themselves to others' expectations of what they ought to do. Their satisfaction comes from living in the present, pursuing their own interests. They're also adaptive enough to change course if at some point they find the path they're on is not where they want to be heading. In fact, if your college degree gives you anything, it ought to be the creativity and adaptability to shift direction if you wish.

Career Services

I know it's a lot easier to sit here giving this advice than to put it into practice. And "practice" is the key word. As a soon-to-be college graduate, you're not only practicing these skills now, but, like most of us, you'll also be practicing these concepts and advice for most of your lives. Fortunately, you're likely to have help on campus. Most schools have trained career counselors, usually available in a career-services office, who can guide you in investigating options, thinking through your choices, and taking steps to find a meaningful position.

Among other things, the career office should be able to put you in touch with alumni from your school working in professions of interest to you. There is no better way of getting a taste of a possible career—and making contacts in that field—than conducting "informational interviews" with alumni. In an informational interview, you'll meet with someone for thirty to sixty minutes to talk to about what he does, what he finds interesting or challenging about his job, and how he got his start. If the meeting goes well, you may even ask him for names of others in their field whom you might call. The beauty of the informational interview is that you remove the pressure of job seeking by asking people about what they do rather than pleading for a job. Most folks love talking about themselves, especially to an aspiring student from their alma mater, and in the process you've made a contact that you can call on if or when you actually decide to seek a job in that field. If you hit it off with the interviewees, they may even take you under their wing to connect you to others who may have open positions.

Another great option is to pursue an internship while in college. Here, your career-services office, major department, or even professors may know of organizations that utilize interns. At the schools where I have taught, I have seen student internships in organizations as varied as newspapers, major engineering and computer companies, consulting firms, political campaigns, hospitals, and international aid groups. As an intern, you likely will not get paid for your work, but at some schools it's possible to earn course credit for the internship, especially if you follow up the experience with a paper. Either way, as an intern you get a window into life in that organization or field while allowing you an opportunity to prove what you can do. I know of many students who landed their first job through an internship, seizing the chance to make themselves indispensible to their employers. Other students have used an internship as an opportunity to build work experience in a field that they can market to other employers.

Keeping It in Perspective

Even as I give this advice, I don't want to worry you too much about life after college. There will be plenty of time to prepare for that. For now, concentrate on enjoying and getting the most out of college life, both in the classroom and in your extracurricular activities. Still, there is always a contingent of students that begins college with a single-minded focus on preprofessional pursuits. Many describe themselves as premed or pre-law, although there are others that enter college convinced they are destined to a particular career. To these students I'm tempted to issue a blanket message of "just relax" as the antidote to overly developed career ambition. But experience tells me that anxiety is not easily addressed by simplistic sayings, and, more to the point, I'm convinced that many of these students believe they're just well focused, not excessively narrow.

In either event, my advice for the preprofessional student is not that different from my overall message about college. Whether you're certain about your postcollege plans or still wondering if you should enroll, there are five key points to keep in mind as you wind your way through college.

Rule 1—Study What Interests You

Contrary to anything else you may have heard, there is no magic major for admission to medical or law school. Although medical schools seek a small set of required classes in the natural sciences—for example, that heartbreaker of a course, organic chemistry—graduate and professional schools seek diversity of interests among their applicants. Employers, too, want creative, responsible, and capable new hires, not necessarily graduates of particular majors. So study what you love as an undergraduate, knowing that if you have excelled at your classes you have created the greatest opportunities for yourself postgraduation.

Rule 2—Push Yourself

No matter your major, take a challenging set of classes. Graduate schools and employers want students with exceptional reading, analytical, and writing skills. You won't build these abilities by racking up multiple introductory classes. Dive deep into your schools' curriculum and take opportunities to challenge and prove yourself.

Rule 3—Know Your Faculty

Make professional connections with your faculty so that they will be able to provide strong references for you. As I've said in a prior chapter, it's not useful to garner letters of recommendation that describe you generically—the kind of letter that is written when students haven't distinguished themselves to their professors. Instead, make a point early in your college career of attending office hours, selecting follow-up courses from professors you like and admire, and volunteering for research projects run by your professors. In addition to building the kind of professional relationships that make college more rewarding, these connections are the natural prerequisites to strong letters of recommendation that say something significant about your interests and abilities.

Rule 4—Learn Outside of the Classroom

Do something—anything—besides limiting yourself to your studies. As much as graduate schools and employers seek academically superior students, they also want students who will be interesting and effective contributors to their professions. Just think of your own experience with doctors. With whom would you be most comfortable discussing that embarrassing skin condition—the doctor who understands cell division but can't relate to patients, or the physician who has outside interests and can relate to your references? But don't see this advice simply as an instrumental strategy for admission to graduate school. Pursuing extracurricular interests in college will expand your life and make school more enjoyable. Even as I urge you to concentrate on your studies—and, frankly, wouldn't we all be surprised if your professors told you to slack off from classwork?—make sure that you achieve some balance in your life. All work and no play not only makes you boring, but it also wastes the many opportunities outside of class to enjoy yourself and grow as a person.

Rule 5—Investigate Your Options

At some point during college I'm sure you will hear someone say that a master's degree is the new bachelor's degree, that you need graduate study to make yourself attractive in a competitive job market. To be sure, there are a few professions that require an advanced degree, and we can likely name them on one or two hands: law, medicine, dentistry, veterinary medicine, and academe. But that's about it. In any other field, you make your path as you go. For that matter, you ought to think quite carefully before committing to several years of graduate or professional school. At more than $25,000 per year, are you prepared to go into substantial debt for a field you may or may not want to pursue? As a "recovering lawyer" myself, I see the pile of law degrees discarded by law school graduates who are no longer practicing law. Was that law degree needed to help people get to their present positions? Perhaps. But in many cases I'm confident that these law grads could have had as rewarding, interesting, and lucrative a career without spending the three years and thousands upon thousands of dollars to attend law school. As I tell my undergraduates, if you want to be a lawyer, then by all means go to law school. But if you have any doubts, wait it out until you've truly investigated your career options.

Apart from a professional program like law or medicine, will a general graduate degree be helpful in a career? Yes, in most circumstances, if only because you will have expanded and deepened your knowledge of a field. But a master's degree is rarely a prerequisite for career advancement. Just take a look at the list of CEOs in the industries that interest you and trace their career paths. Undoubtedly, some have graduate degrees, but those were not the source of their career advancement. Rather, the people who have risen to the top were those who prepared well, worked hard, and were willing to take some risks. I know I'm sounding like a broken record, but I have to keep saying this to ensure that you finish this book with the point firmly in mind.

The Most Important Rule—Make Your Own Path

In a world in which college preparation has become more of a business, where students and their parents are seeking certainty that the investment of time and money in college will pay off, I see more and more students who are looking for a singular path to "success," however that ephemeral term is defined. But it's not that simple, which, thankfully, is the good news. The key to *your* career satisfaction, to your personal success, will be as unique as you are. Whether it's now before you graduate or twenty years down the road once you have had some more ups and downs from life, you will come to realize that the only person you need to impress is yourself and that the one person who must live with your choices is you.

Life has a way of evening out who is ahead and who has supposedly failed. Just ask anyone who has returned from her twenty-fifth high school reunion. Two decades from now, you and most of your classmates will have acted on life, and life will have acted on you. When you hit that point, looking back on the path you have taken since college, I can promise you that you will be most satisfied in both your professional and personal life if you have followed what spoke to you, not done things you felt you were supposed to accomplish. As trite as it may sound, there is no manual for life and no "right" path.

Let me close with advice that I first read in the alumni magazine of my alma mater, the College of Literature, Science, and the Arts at the University of Michigan. In answering the question "What do you want to do with your life?" that magazine offered the following prophetic response that neatly encapsulates much of what I've been urging:

> Understand that you won't know what you want to do and what you're able to do until you try doing lots of things. Recognize that if you pour yourself into each thing you try, your time will never be wasted. Don't worry too much. Don't be too hard on yourself. Remember that the folks that seem like they've got it all figured out don't really have it all figured out, or okay, even if they do, that's all right, because your path is different, and its unpredictability—despite the anxieties that creates—is a gift. Don't be pulled in by anyone else's ideas of success—do what you want to do, and be what you want to be. Be open. Allow for serendipity.[4]

If you can do this, if you take on the challenge of college life with your eyes open, considering the several options available to you and weighing the choices against your interests, then your college degree with truly be worth the time and effort you have poured into it. Ultimately, what we're trying to teach you in college is a philosophy for approaching your adult years, a set of skills that will maintain your intellectual curiosity while opening you to new ideas and experiences. If you can accomplish that while maintaining a core sense of your values, then you will be a success no matter where you have gone to school or what you do afterwards. As your professors, we're ready and excited to help. The opportunity is yours. Make the most of college.

NOTES

CHAPTER 1

1. U.S. Census Bureau News, "College Degree Nearly Doubles Annual Earnings, Census Bureau Reports," March 28, 2005, accessed December 11, 2008, http://usgovinfo.about.com/od/censusandstatistics/a/collegepays.htm.

2. "Fast Facts," National Center for Education Statistics, accessed June 16, 2011, http://nces.ed.gov/fastfacts/display.asp?id=98.

3. Frank H. T. Rhodes, "After 40 Years of Growth and Change, Higher Education Faces New Challenges," *Chronicle of Higher Education*, November 24, 2006, accessed August 9, 2011, http://chronicle.com/weekly/v53/i14/14a01801.htm.

4. Ibid.

5. Jeffrey Thomas, "International Student Enrollment at U.S. Colleges Breaks Record: Official Says State Department Committed to Welcoming Foreign Students," America.gov., November 18, 2008, accessed December 11, 2008, http://www.america.gov/st/educ-english/2008/November/200811171600491CJsamohTo.646908.html.

6. U.S. Census Bureau News, "College Degree Nearly Doubles Annual Earnings."

7. Marty Nemko, "America's Most Overrated Product: The Bachelor's Degree," *Chronicle of Higher Education*, May 2, 2008, http://chronicle.com/article/America-s-Most-Overrated/19869.

8. Associated Press, "Survey: Students Stop, Slow Degree Work due to Economy," *USA Today*, October 22, 2008, accessed December 11, 2008, http://www.usatoday.com/news/education/2008–10–21-college-loans_N.htm.

9. Barack Obama, speech to the Democratic National Convention, July 27, 2004, accessed December 13, 2008, http://www.americanrhetoric.com/speeches/convention2004/barackobama2004dnc.htm.

10. Jacques Steinberg, "Don't Worry, Be Students," September 30, 2007, accessed August 9, 2011, http://www.nytimes.com/2007/09/30/magazine/30poll-t.html?pagewanted=print.

11. According to Nemko, only 23 percent of the 1.3 million high school graduates of 2007 who took the ACT examination were ready for college-level work in the core subjects of English, math, reading, and science (Nemko, "America's Most Overrated Product").

CHAPTER 2

1. As of 2008, for-profit schools constituted 8 percent of student enrollment in colleges eligible for financial aid (Rhodes, "After 40 Years of Growth and Change, Higher Education Faces New Challenges").

2. Rachel Aviv, "Strategy Adult Ed.," *New York Times Education Life*, November 2, 2008, 6.

CHAPTER 3

1. Fred Topel, "Dish Talks to Woody Allen," *Dish Magazine*, accessed March 24, 2011, http://dishmag.com/issue84/celebrity/8350/dish-talks-to-woody-allen/.

2. NDT Resource Center, "Understanding Different Learning Styles," accessed December 23, 2010, http://www.ndt-ed.org/TeachingResources/ClassroomTips/Learning_Styles.htm.

CHAPTER 4

1. "A as the New B." *New York Times*, April 18, 2010, accessed December 23, 2010, http://www.nytimes.com/imagepages/2010/04/18/education/edlife/20100418-Edlife-Data-gr.html?src=tptw.

2. Alicia C. Shepard, "A's for Everyone!" *Washington Post*, June 5, 2005, accessed December 23, 2010, http://www.washingtonpost.com/wp-dyn/content/article/2005/06/02/AR2005060201593.html; Stuart Rojstaczer, "Grade Inflation Gone Wild," *Christian Science Monitor*, March 24, 2009, accessed December 23, 2010, http://www.csmonitor.com/Commentary/Opinion/2009/0324/p09s02-coop.html.

3. Benjamin S. Bloom, *Taxonomy of Educational Objectives, Handbook 1: Cognitive Domain* (New York: David McKay Co., 1956).

4. Lorin Anderson and David Krathwohl, eds., *A Taxonomy for Learning, Teaching, and Assessing: A Revision of Bloom's Taxonomy of Educational Objectives* (New York: Longman, 2001); David Krathwohl, "A Revision of Bloom's Taxonomy: An Overview," *Theory into Practice* 41 (2002): 212–18.

5. Lucy C. Jacobs, "How to Write Better Tests: A Handbook for Improving Test Construction Skills," IUB Evaluation Services & Testing, accessed December 23, 2010, http://www.indiana.edu/~best/write_better_tests.shtml.

6. Robert Runté, "Test Wise Tricks" (student handout, 1995), accessed December 23, 2010, http://www.uleth.ca/edu/runte/tests/take/mc/how.html#Tricks.

7. Joshua S. Rubinstein, David E. Meyer, and Jeffrey E. Evans, "Executive Control of Cognitive Processes in Task Switching," *Journal of Experimental Psychology: Human Perception and Performance* 27 (2001): 763–97.

8. Matt Richtel, "Your Brain on Computers: Attached to Technology and Paying a Price," *New York Times*, June 6, 2010, accessed December 23, 2010, http://www.nytimes.com/2010/06/07/technology/07brain.html?_r=1.

9. Facts About Sleep," campusmindworks, accessed December 23, 2010, http://www.campusmindworks.org/students/self_care/sleep.asp.

10. "Sleep," Nova Science Now, accessed December 23, 2010, http://www.pbs.org/wgbh/nova/body/sleep.html.

11. Kendra Davis and Mike Martinoli, "Red Bull gives you . . . a) tremors b) anxiety c) insomnia d) all the above." *The Villanovan*, February 10, 2010, ac-

cessed December 23, 2010, http://www.villanovan.com/features/red-bull-gives-you-a-tremors-b-anxiety-c-insomnia-d-all-the-above-1.1123462.

12. Joan Oleck, "Most High School Students Admit to Cheating." *School Library Journal*, March 10, 2008, accessed December 23, 2010, http://www.schoollibrary journal.com/article/CA6539855.html; Emily Sachar, "60% of U.S. High School Students Cheat, 28% Steal, Study Finds." Bloomberg News, October 14, 2006, accessed December 15, 2010, http://www.bloomberg.com/apps/news?pid=news archive&sid=aYvMinAiKtPk.

CHAPTER **5**

1. Valerie Strauss, "The Rich Irony in Virginia's History Textbook Error," Answer Sheet, *Washington Post*, October 20, 2010, accessed October 22, 2010, http://voices.washingtonpost.com/answer-sheet/curriculum/the-rich-irony-in-virginias-hi.html.

2. Kevin Sieff, "Virginia 4th-Grade Textbook Criticized over Claims on Black Confederate Soldiers." *Washington Post,* October 20, 2010. accessed October 22, 2010, http://www.washingtonpost.com/wp-dyn/content/article/2010/10/19/AR2010101907974.html?hpid=topnews.

3. Ibid.

4. Ibid.

5. The process is called double-blind, because neither authors nor reviewers are privy to each other's identity. At the time a work is published, the reviewers are able to figure out the identity of the authors, but unless reviewers later reveal themselves to the authors (and many do not), the authors will never know the identity of the individuals who reviewed their work.

6. "Al Franken Quotes," Al Franken Sense, accessed November 17, 2010, http://www.alfrankensense.com/al_franken_quotes.html.

7. Allen Guttman, "From *Typee* to *Moby Dick*: Melville's Allusive Art," *Modern Language Quarterly* 24, no. 3 (1963): 237–44, accessed October 27, 2010, http://mlq.dukejournals.org/cgi/pdf_extract/24/3/237.

8. "Biblical and Mythological Allusions in *Moby Dick*," 123helpme.com, accessed October 27, 2010, http://www.123helpme.com/view.asp?id=3727.

9. "About ICPSR," Inter-University Consortium for Political and Social Research, accessed October 27, 2010, http://www.icpsr.umich.edu/icpsrweb/ICPSR/org/index.jsp;jsessionid=D40CC3461CB5B772F72C4517CFC1FF96.

10. "Writing Tips," Hamilton, accessed November 1, 2010, http://www.hamilton.edu/tip.

11. A good example of such a website can be found at Hamilton College: http://www.hamlton.edu/tip.

12. Eberly Center for Teaching Excellence and Intercultural Communication Center, "Recognizing and Addressing Cultural Variations in the Classroom," accessed November 2, 2010, http://www.cmu.edu/teaching/resources/Publica tionsArchives/InternalReports/culturalvariations.pdf.

13. William Shakespeare, *Hamlet*, act 3, sc. 1.

14. One of them, in fact, brazenly penned an article for the *Chronicle of Higher Education* in 2010, claiming that he had earned $66,000 per year writing papers for students (Ed Dante, "The Shadow Scholar," *Chronicle of Higher Education*, November 12, 2010, accessed December 14, 2010, http://chronicle.com/article/The-Shadow-Scholar/125329/).

15. His experience is emblematic of businesses like R2C2, which search for papers available online and then sell them to other students as original work. Interestingly, in September 2010, R2C2 settled a class-action lawsuit against its practices, agreeing to shut down its websites and exit the term-paper business (Paige Chapman, "Settlement Reached in Essay-Mill Lawsuit," *Chronicle of Higher Education*, October 25, 2010, accessed December 14, 2010, http://chronicle.com/blogs/wiredcampus/settlement-reached-in-essay-mill-lawsuit/27852).

CHAPTER **6**

1. E. Frank Stephenson, "Is this Exam Hazardous to Your Grandmother's Health?" *Atlantic Economic Journal* 31(2003): 384.

2. "Marijuana Facts and Figures," Office of National Drug Control Policy, accessed March 2, 2011, http://www.whitehousedrugpolicy.gov/drugfact/marijuana/marijuana_ff.html.

3. The columnist and author, John Feinstein, regularly derides the NCAA for this designation, considering it a myth for an organization that is obsessed with making money (Feinstein, "A Basketball Tournament only the NCAA Would Love," *Washington Post*, April 6, 2010).

4. "How to Survive Grown-Ups Asking You What Your Plans Are When You Have No Idea What Your Plans Are." *LSA Magazine*, Spring 2009, 30.

INDEX

academic advisors, 33, 36, 78
academic dishonesty. *See* cheating; plagiarism
academic integrity policies, 133
academic journals. *See* scholarly journals
academic probation, 135
academic problems, 137; and counseling, 142–43; grade appeals, 144–46; health and family emergencies, 141–42; skills deficiency, 138–40; and student athletes, 146–50; and substance abuse, 143–44
academic skills, 138–40
active reading, 138
active studying, 91
adjunct faculty, 21, 22
advanced placement courses, 37–38
alcohol on campus, 143–44. *See also* substance abuse
Allen, Woody, 50
alternative major, 35
Americans with Disabilities Act, 140
analysis, in writing process, 123, 124–25
analyzing, as learning objective, 83, 84, 99
anxiety, 143
application, as learning objective, 83, 84, 99
argumentative writing, 86
athletic department tutoring, 149, 150
athletic scholarships, 146–47

Beck, Glenn, 113
Belushi, John, 12
Biblioscape, 121
Blackboard, 52

Bloom, Benjamin, 83
blue books, 94
Brandeis, Louis, 126

caffeine, 94, 160n11
capstone classes, 24, 48
career decisions, 152; and informational interviews with alumni, 153; and internships, 153
career services, 152–53
caveat emptor, 22
challenge: challenging one's self, 154; challenging one's views, 16–18
cheating, 95, 102–5; consequences of, 103–4; and self-respect, 105. *See also* plagiarism
citation: and plagiarism, 131–33; rules of, 131–32; styles, 132–33
citation styles: American Medical Association, 132; American Psychological Association, 132; Turabian, 132; University of Chicago Press, 132
class attendance, 24, 50–52, 65
classes: sleeping in, 53–54; where to sit, 52–54
class participation, 25, 65–69; art of, 68–69; asking questions, 66–67; reasons for, 67–68
class schedules, 11
class size, 19, 48
closed book test, 81
closing, of paper, 123
coasting, postgraduation, 150–51
college: differences from high school, 11–13; paths to, 10; reasons for attending, 7–8; value of, 9–10

college enrollment: of African Americans, 7; of foreign students, 7; at state institutions, 7; of women, 7

college graduation, and career success, 8

college graduation rates, 7

college preparation: cottage industry, 1–2; guidebooks, 2; options for unprepared students, 10; proportion of high school graduates prepared for college, 159n11

college professors. *See* faculty

college reputation, 38

community colleges, 10

confusion, admitting, 25–26

core course requirements, 28, 32

Coulter, Ann, 113

Council for Adult and Experiential Learning, 40

counseling, 142–43, 144

course identification number, 32

course load, 11, 37

course preparation, 12, 25, 58; anticipating questions, 61–62; keeping up with readings, 58

courses: normal meeting schedule, 52; progressive pattern of, 49; readings, 54–55

course selection, 28–32; and interest, 29–30

course withdrawal, 142

credit hour, 11

critical thinking, 16, 17, 35

databases, 118, 119–20

"delayed adolescence," 151

Dell, Michael, 8

discussion, in paper writing, 123, 124

discussion sections, 47, 49, 66; note taking in, 63

distance learning, 38–40

distribution requirements, 32

diversity on campus, 7, 11

double-blind peer-review process, 112, 161n5

double major, 35

drugs on campus: marijuana, 144. *See also* substance abuse

"dumbing down," of high school education, 138

early graduation, 37–38

earnings, of college graduates relative to non-attendees, 8

editing, in writing process, 105, 108, 126–28; editing for grammar, 128–29

editing services, 138

electronic research databases, 118, 119–20

Ellison, Larry, 8

e-mail, and communicating with professors, 72–73

EndNote, 121

entry-level career positions, 150, 151

essay questions, types of, 87

essay tests, 82, 86–88; application of six levels of cognitive thought in, 99; how to answer, 98–101; outlining answers, 101; timing of, 101

esteem, 10

evaluation, as learning objective, 83, 84, 99

examinations. *See* tests

experiential education, 40–41

expository writing, 86

expulsion, 135

extracurricular activities, 36, 155

face-to-face discussion, 39–40

faculty: earnings, 15; English-language proficiency, 20; getting the most from, 24–27; ideology, 15; and professional friendship, 26; qualifications, 20; teaching preparation, 12–14; ways of contacting, 72–73

faculty roles, 14–15, 19; academic advising, 36; mentoring, 26, 70;

learning objectives, Bloom's taxonomy of, 83–84

learning-skills centers, 10, 138–39, 149, 150

lecture courses, 45–46, 50; note taking in, 63

lecture-discussion classes, 45, 47–48

letters of recommendation, 26, 35, 70–72, 155

liberal arts, defined, 29

liberal arts colleges, 29; and faculty teaching role, 12, 48

literature review, 123

major: alternative, 35; defined, 33; double major, 35; process of choosing, 33–35; when to choose, 33

make-up exams, 148

mentoring, 26, 70

midterm examination, 91

minor, 35

Modern Language Association citation style, 132

motivation, 10

multiple-choice and true-false tests, 82, 84–85; advantages and disadvantages of, 86; changing answers, 97; how to answer, 97–98

multiple-choice questions: "all/none of the above" options, 97; examples of, 85

multitasking, 92–93

NCAA, 146, 147, 162n3

news magazines, 119

newspapers, 119

non–tenure-track faculty, 19, 20

notes: borrowing, 52, 65; and definitions, 64; synthesizing, 64–65

note taking: in classroom, 62–65; and learning-skills programs, 138; in lectures, 63; in seminars or discussion sections, 63; while reading, 58–61

note-taking programs, 121

Obama, Barack, 9

office hours, utilizing, 26–27; and academic problems, 137, 139; and getting your money's worth, 69–70; and grade appeals, 145, 146; and letters of recommendation, 70–72, 155; and personal attention from instructors, 49; and student athletes, 149–50

Olbermann, Keith, 113–14

online courses, 39–40

online searches and databases, 117, 118, 119–20

open book tests, 82

optional reading, 57

O'Reilly, Bill, 113

papers, writing. *See* writing papers

paraphrasing, 132, 133

parents: concerns about "partying," 11, 12; influence on preparation for college, 30, 36, 80; overprotective, 31, 135; and paying for college, 2, 8, 31, 151; and pressure to study a "practical" field, 30, 34

PEAR (position, explain, alternative views, responding to possible objections), 124

peer-reviewed journals, 14, 118

peer-review process, 112

peer tutoring, 138

personal problems, 137

physical disabilities, 140

plagiarism, 120–21; and citation, 131–33; ease of detection, 134; and editing assistance, 135; as insult to professors, 135–36; penalties for, 135; purchased papers, 134–35, 162n14, 162n15; stealth, 133

popular media, and research, 117, 119

postgraduation, 150–52; investigating options, 155–56; making one's own path, 156–57

PowerPoint presentations, 52